MANAGING
NEW-PRODUCT
DEVELOPMENT

—MANAGING—
NEW-PRODUCT
DEVELOPMENT

Geoff Vincent

VNR VAN NOSTRAND REINHOLD
_____ New York

Copyright © 1989 by Geoff Vincent

Library of Congress Catalog Card Number 88-33083
ISBN 0-442-23808-8

First published in Great Britain by
Kogan Page Ltd, 120 Pentonville Road
London N1 9JN

Published in the United States of America by
Van Nostrand Reinhold
115 Fifth Avenue
New York, New York 10003

Distributed in Canada by
Macmillan of Canada
Division of Canada Publishing Corporation
164 Commander Boulevard
Agincourt, Ontario M1S 3C7, Canada

16 15 14 13 12 11 10 9 8 7 6 5 4 3 2 1

Library of Congress Cataloging-in-Publication Data

Vincent, Geoff.
  Managing new-product development / Geoff Vincent.
    p.   cm.
  Includes index.
  ISBN 0-442-23808-8
  1. New products—Management. 2. Product management. I. Title.
HF5415.153.V56   1989
658.5'75—dc19   88-33083
                                                                CIP

Printed and bound in Great Britain

CONTENTS

ACKNOWLEDGEMENTS

I have been fortunate enough to observe, participate in and lead projects in a variety of industries and in many different types of organisation. I am indebted for practical ideas, experience and example to present and former colleagues at PA Technology, Philips, Texas Instruments, Acorn Computer and elsewhere. I must mention especially David Lowdell and John Anderson.

I must also thank my wife Franni for extreme patience, valuable suggestions, ruthless criticism and frequent cups of coffee. I dedicate this book to her.

Geoff Vincent
January 1988

1 INTRODUCTION: OPPORTUNITY, RISK AND BENEFIT

This book is about development. Development is the means by which technology is applied to the needs of business, and of society in general. In a competitive climate, it is something that no company can afford to ignore.

New technology has changed the shape of every business activity, from banking to agriculture. Technology underpins every business, but it is not easy to control. For this reason many have simply avoided the issue. Others have taken the plunge, with varying results. Yet there are some basic rules and techniques which, while not guaranteeing success, nevertheless make development manageable in the same way as other business functions.

These basic rules and techniques will be presented in this book. It is written for everyone interested in the application of technology, but especially for two groups of people. First, for those who lead development projects. They may start out as technologists but have to learn project management the hard way; or they may be experienced managers having to face the special problems of technology. Unfortunately, the most common training method for project leaders is still bitter experience.

It is also written for senior managers, and others in a position to commission development projects. Project leaders cannot succeed alone. They need the backing of an organisation which understands how development works and is prepared to make the management decisions necessary to promote a successful outcome.

This book is derived from the practical experience of running development projects, large and small, in some of the fastest moving of present day industries, including electronics, personal computers, telecommunications and print. It is not intended to be a theoretical exposition, but to give practical advice and a flavour of what it takes to run successful projects.

In the modern environment of competition, from home and abroad, companies must adopt a competitive approach to development. What is needed is a fast-track route based on a true understanding of what is involved, with the backup of policy decisions designed to support development activity. Development is one of the last functions to be fully integrated into the mainstream of business life. Yet it has never before been so crucial to success.

How to read this book

Chapter 2 sets the framework for development. It describes the life history of a development project and how it can be divided into distinct phases with specific aims.

Chapter 3 covers the crucial period of setting up a project: defining the requirement, setting appropriate goals and building an effective project team.

Chapter 4 addresses planning. This is a vital skill – both for setting the direction of a project, and for monitoring progress – and one that is rarely used to its full potential.

Chapter 5 discusses the specific issues of organisation and administration that often make the difference between smooth progress and frustrated delay.

Chapter 6 tackles cost and time.

Finally, Chapter 7 describes the particular issues that arise in managing specific technologies.

To a large extent the chapters can be read in isolation, although Chapter 2 establishes a frame of reference that puts much of the later material in context.

The remainder of this introduction addresses some of the business issues that surround development, and that are inevitably the driving force behind it.

MARKET OPPORTUNITIES

Every development project starts with the perception of an opportunity. The better this is characterised, the easier it will be to judge the levels of expenditure and risk that are justified.

There are some characteristic patterns by which technology creates new products and new services. Identifying these patterns and exploiting them early gives a company a significant competitive advantage.

Always, there are two factors to be considered: market trends, and technology opportunities. A significant movement in either of these – or sometimes, a slow change which finally crosses the barrier of economic feasibility – can create a new business opportunity.

Often, the injection of technology to an existing business will lead to a more effective product or service (Fig 1.1).

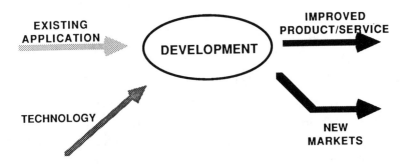

Figure 1.1 Technology injection

Technology can make an existing product cheaper; it can also make it easier to use. The advent of desktop publishing means that firms of all sizes, as well as journalists and other professionals, can now produce their own high quality leaflets, reports and even books. The DIY market has been created from nothing by a combination of increased spending power and leisure time with technical improvements that have made a wide variety of products accessible to the amateur.

A completely new opportunity can arise when two or more technologies converge to make possible a novel application (Fig 1.2).

A classic example of this is the personal computer industry. Computer technology had been well developed, researched and understood. It was applied in certain well-defined areas such as accounting and scientific research. Advances in semiconductor technology (in particular, the integrated circuit) suddenly made computer power available at a fraction of its previous cost.

To exploit the new possibilities, there had to be developments in the way computers were built, in the way they interacted with

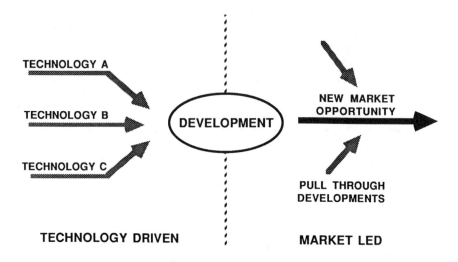

Figure 1.2 Technology convergence

users, and in the application software in order to make them usable to a wider market. These developments were pulled through by the new market opportunities which were opening up. The business rapidly changed from being technology-driven to being market-led.

Companies such as Apple, Sinclair, Acorn and, later, IBM made the most of these possibilities – some of which developed in unexpected ways. IBM now makes more money from personal computers than from any other source. A single software application – the spreadsheet – has generated millions of sales worldwide. More recently, desktop publishing has been a major growth area, spearheaded by Apple and the Macintosh computer, with IBM running hard to make up lost ground.

The microcomputer has also found its way into all types of control applications, from washing machines to complete factories. It has pulled through development in many other areas, such as cheap information storage (magnetic and optical discs) and flat panel displays. It has also had a major impact on communications, encouraging the switch from analogue to digital techniques. Many modern developments, from space technology to advanced navigation methods, and from medical diagnostic equipment to 24-hour banking, would be impossible without it.

The microcomputer represents a key enabling technology, because it has spawned a host of subsidiary applications in

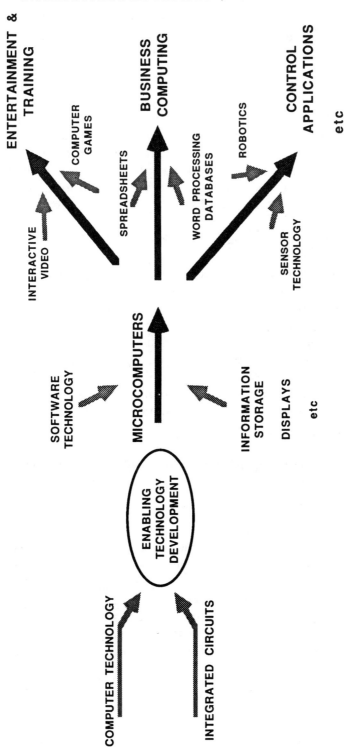

Figure 1.3 An enabling technology

diverse areas, many of which have grown into major businesses.

This enabling technology has been compared with others in history, such as the invention of printing, or even of writing itself. But microcomputers are not the only example of this effect. There are many similar cases, on a smaller scale and with more localised application. Spotting such key opportunities is a vital skill for all types of business, whether to identify opportunities for exploitation or to predict likely competition.

Since technology usually takes a number of years to emerge from the laboratory to the high street (or factory, or office), the chances of a correct prediction are better for those who have access to recent research and development, and can match this with knowledge of relevant market behaviour.

Exploiting an enabling technology can be very profitable, if done in the right way. The development period can be long and sometimes difficult, because significant new principles are at stake. But launch of the basic product can be followed up quickly with subsidiary projects. There is a large initial investment hump, but subsidiary developments should show a small additional investment leading to a rapid and profitable return.

What it takes to identify and exploit opportunities of this and other kinds is an ear to the ground in the key areas of market trends and new technical developments. This can be done on a continuous basis, or as a commissioned survey at a particular moment. Such vigilance is a worthwhile insurance policy against the unexpected discovery of a competitive product that changes long standing rules of price or marketing. Recent history shows that it does not take long for a well established industry to undergo a complete and drastic reversal.

Some companies reach a position where their traditional market – or one of their markets – is in long term decline, and they need to break out into new fields. In this case, it helps to gain an outside view. There are some standard methods for addressing this situation which have been proven in practice. They usually amount to a structured way of gathering ideas and opinions from a wide range of experts inside and outside the company, and matching these with the strengths and capabilities available. It is not unusual for a company to be reborn with greater strength than before. What is certain is that many more companies are having to face up to this type of re-examination.

RISK VERSUS BENEFIT

Development is an activity that inevitably involves risk. Risk can never be eliminated, but it can be understood, evaluated and managed. Development risk always has to be balanced against the certainty that, without it, every business will sooner or later be overtaken by the competition.

A graph of the real benefit obtained from a typical project versus the innovative risk taken would look something like Fig 1.4:

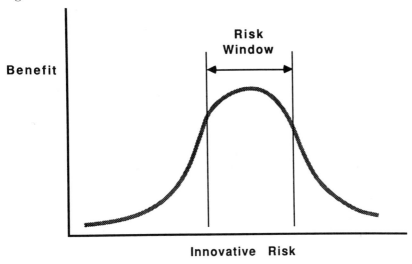

Figure 1.4 Benefit versus risk

A more challenging development, if it succeeds and assuming it is well targeted, is likely to bring higher rewards. However, a high risk project stands more chance of failing due to inherent technical or marketing difficulties. A low risk project is likely to succeed 99 times out of 100, but the rewards will be small. There is a risk window which represents the best value investment for the business. Obviously, it is worth asking whether the risk being taken on a project is too high. Not so obvious is the question whether the innovative risk being taken is too low to be worthwhile.

There is a type of risk, of course, which can and should be eliminated: the avoidable risk due to bad project management or poor technical skills. But there is a fundamental risk associated with developing something new, just as there is a risk associated with entering a new market or taking on new people. It is this which must be understood, and compared with potential benefits, in order to target development effectively.

Risk, like timescale and budget, is one of the key project parameters that need to be communicated to senior management, both at the start of a project and throughout its life. Unfortunately, it cannot be reduced to a single figure. But a feel for the key risk areas of a project, and the level of difficulty in each, can be conveyed by the project leader – particularly if he or she submits regular reports and builds an effective relationship with whoever is commissioning the project. Risk is a key factor in making appropriate business decisions, and an effective way needs to be found to communicate it. Too much information can easily obscure the key issues – which usually boil down to a small number of critical activities.

Sometimes it is worthwhile to bring in independent reviewers – from inside or outside the organisation – to take a fresh look at a project and provide a second opinion. Once identified, of course, it is possible to deal with the risk areas. A well managed project will, wherever possible, tackle the key risks first, so that the level of risk decreases rapidly as the project progresses.

TIMING

Fig 1.5 shows a typical cash flow curve for a development project. Expenditure is low at the idea and feasibility stages, but rapidly climbs during development. If the market has been judged correctly, and advertising and distribution do their job,

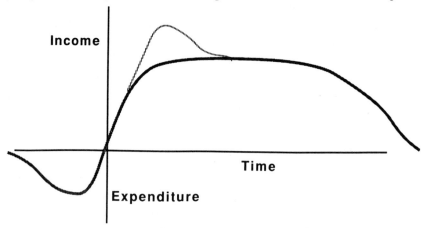

Figure 1.5 Development cash flow

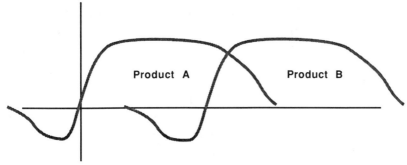

Figure 1.6 Successful development timing

sales income should rise quickly to a peak. Typically it will flatten out for a period and then start to decline, due to competition or market saturation. Sometimes, there is a novelty effect: an early peak, which settles down to a lower plateau. For the project to be worthwhile, of course, the positive part of the curve must provide adequate return on the development expenditure.

How long this cycle is depends on the industry. The common factor in almost every industry, however, is that the cycle is getting shorter. It used to be the case that a business could survive on the flat part of the curve for a generation or more, and in effect ignore the issue of development. That is no longer so.

There *are* things that can be done to prolong the life of a product: better marketing, for example, or expansion into new markets. But eventually it will be necessary to introduce something new.

Fig 1.6 shows an example of successful timing. Research and development expenditure is supported by the top of the sales curve, and the new product is introduced just as sales of the old one begin to drop in earnest. This is a picture to keep investors happy.

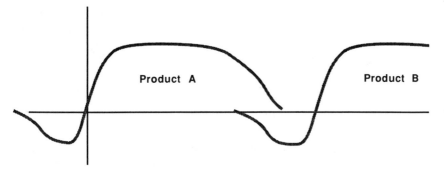

Figure 1.7 Product gap

Fig 1.7 shows a less fortunate situation. Not only are sales of Product A tailing off alarmingly, but there is heavy development expenditure in a desperate attempt to get something (anything) developed in double quick time. If this is a small company, it may never have the chance to complete the job. Even a larger company with several products will experience a significant drop in profits. It is not unknown for a heavy cash drain in one subsidiary to leave a major company wide open to predators.

With a new product development, it is often the case that manufacturing costs fall rapidly after an initial period. This is particularly true of electronic products. Almost certainly, others will seek to take advantage of this and introduce competitive products at a lower price.

It helps to plan product developments on this basis. In fact, there are two options as the basic cost of the technology falls: add more features and retain the price, or reduce the cost and expand the market. Sometimes it is possible to do both, and produce a range of products. What is not possible in a competitive environment is to stand still. In view of development lead times, new projects need to be started while the existing product generation is at the height of its sales potential.

THE COMPETITIVE APPROACH

Most companies are used to competition in the fields of marketing, manufacture and distribution. What has come as a surprise to many is the increased pace of competition in the development of new products and services. It is no longer possible to survive for a decade or more selling the same basic product in the same market. Many businesses now depend for their success, and their survival, on techniques which did not exist 20 or 30 years ago.

This increased rate of new product introduction, particularly from overseas, has altered the business climate. The companies that come out on top will be those that respond quickly and accurately to new market needs and new technical possibilities. They will do this by developing what is wanted in the shortest possible time.

A byproduct of free world trade is that consumers of all kinds are no longer willing to accept obsolete or imperfect products. In the long run (and it may not be so very long), the only alternative to establishing a fast and efficient route to development will be to license technology from outside.

For those intending to stay in the race, the crucial problem is how to develop new products quickly and efficiently, designed to meet a specific market opportunity at a particular moment. Once the rules of development are understood, ways to speed up the process become clear – for example, by carrying out different tasks in parallel, by overlapping phases to some extent, by creating dedicated project teams, and by removing organisational obstacles that slow down the development process.

Some of these techniques (overlap and parallel working, for example) increase risk; others are done at some inconvenience to the rest of the organisation. But the options are there, and must be considered against the overall benefit to the organisation.

For many companies, development is rapidly assuming a higher priority in the list of business functions. This book describes how to translate that new importance into action by strategic decisions at the level of organisational policy, and by tactics in the running of specific projects.

2 CONCEPT TO LAUNCH: THE DEVELOPMENT CYCLE

PROJECT PHASES

Development is not one activity but many. Any project goes through a number of stages, each of which has its own characteristics. Techniques applied to, say, the design stage are not appropriate when it comes to production engineering. Different skills need to be brought in. To be successful, the project needs to be run in different ways at different stages of the process.

The best technique is to recognise the difference between activities and to split the project into a number of distinct phases. This not only divides up the work in a convenient way, it also allows the risk and the finance involved to be controlled effectively. In a well run project, there is a definite breakpoint between each phase where the project is reviewed, the results of the previous phase recorded, and the decision taken whether to proceed to the next.

The end of a phase marks a change in the type of activity and gives a sense of achievement and completion to project members. This is particularly important on a long project. It also allows new skills and fresh blood to be brought in where appropriate and permits weaknesses in previous work to be admitted and corrected (without loss of face) before they become impossible to change. The end of a phase is a convenient point for the next part of the work to be replanned and re-estimated, and for risk and financial benefits to be re-assessed.

Fig. 2.1 shows the major phases of a project.

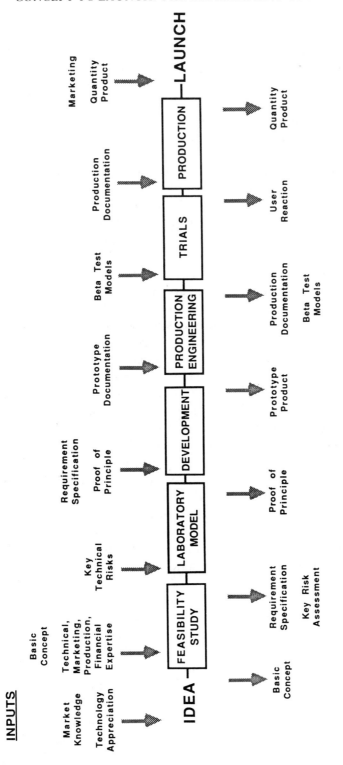

Figure 2.1 The development cycle: major phases

IDEA

The idea for a project may come from anywhere. Often it originates from a technical source, but it may also come from marketing, or senior management, or even from the competition.

Organisations have different attitudes to new ideas. Some stifle them at birth; others take them seriously if they come from some quarters but not from others. The most productive attitude is to consider all ideas, from whatever source, on their merits. Obviously some early filtering will take place, based on perceptions of where previous business has been and what the purpose of the organisation is. But this filtering can often block good business opportunities which do not quite fit into any accepted categories.

The Walkman portable cassette player exists now only because one man believed in the concept in the face of total opposition from the rest of his company. That one man was the chairman of Sony, so he was in the happy position of being able to act on his belief. Other ideas have had a much rougher ride.

Some successful organisations have mechanisms specifically designed to remove the filtering in a controlled way, and allow a fresh look to be taken at what might seem at first sight to be wild ideas. Texas Instruments is one company which deliberately sets aside small sums of money to explore 'wild hares'. The company's very successful educational toys ('Speak and Spell', 'Speak and Math' etc) originated in this way.

Another approach is to hold brainstorm or workshop sessions specifically designed to produce new ideas. This technique can be particularly effective for a company which has an existing range of products coming to the end of their useful life. The company needs to diversify into new products and possibly new markets in order to maintain a healthy cash flow.

FEASIBILITY STUDY

Having produced an idea (or several ideas), it is wise to assess feasibility before spending large sums of money on development. Many people are afraid of development because it appears to involve large expenditure for uncertain reward. But a strictly limited first stage investment can be used to assess the market and address key technical issues before any large commitments are made. This type of positive risk management is of increasing importance to many companies.

A feasibility study in effect conducts the whole project in miniature – mainly on paper, but partly by conducting key experiments and tests. Technical experimentation in the laboratory may be combined with suitably targeted market research. On the marketing side, a full feasibility study should address the type and size of the market, methods of distribution, the economics of the business, likely competition and so on. On the technical side, key risk areas should be explored, comparisions made with previous work, and methods of implementation sketched out. For a new product development, manufacturing issues are also important: how will it be made, where, and in what volume?

The end result of a feasibility study should be a clear assessment of risk and benefit, together with an outline plan for proceeding to the next stage.

Feasibility studies are best carried out by a small team of perhaps two or three people. However, the team should have access to all the skills and expertise that are likely to be employed on the project itself: technical specialists in the relevant disciplines, production engineers, marketing and sales specialists and so on.

A feasibility study should ask all the important questions that will be asked on the project itself. Is this possible? How much will it cost? How long will it take? What skills will be needed? These are some of the technical questions. The marketing questions include, for example: What is the market? How big is it? When is it? What price will it stand? What features does it want? How elastic is the market to changes in price/features/timing etc?

There are also questions of finance and business economics: development cash flow, capital outlay, return on investment, payback period, sensitivity to volume fluctuations etc. All of these questions should receive at least a preliminary answer before the real money is spent.

There is often a temptation to cut back on the feasibility study – either not to do it, or to skimp on some aspects. This is false economy. It is unfortunately all too easy to list projects where, several million pounds down the road, the organisation concerned wishes it had spent a few thousand resolving (for example) exactly what the market really wants. A good feasibility study not only weeds out bad ideas, it also spies out the ground, identifies blind alleys, and directs the project towards terra firma (both in a technical and a marketing sense). A development project is not unlike a military campaign: reconnaissance pays great dividends.

Output
The output of a feasibility study is likely to be two things:

1. A report on the study covering issues addressed, questions answered, blind alleys explored, and conclusions.
2. A first draft requirements specification, setting out the need for what is being developed and the basic features required, in language that can be understood by all involved in the project, whether salesmen, businessmen or technologists.

The report is a matter of historical record, setting out the findings so far, recommendations for action and the reasons for them. It is a document for immediate consumption: it should be considered and acted on. Once this has been done, its function is complete.

The requirements specification has a longer life. It should be the first element in a 'live' hierarchy of specifications that will be maintained and referred to throughout the project. It defines the ultimate goal of the project, and its existence is the first means of ensuring that everyone in the project is pulling in the same direction. Specifications are discussed further below (Chapter 3 and Chapter 5).

LABORATORY MODEL

A laboratory model is a first attempt to produce a working example of the product or system – or at least something closely related to it. It is a proof that the concept works in physical reality rather than on paper. However, it may look nothing like the final product. Projects involving electronics may have racks full of components, or perhaps a computer, in place of a chip yet to be developed. Mechanisms may be crude and made from the wrong materials. The system may be the wrong size. Features may be lacking, and it will almost certainly need experts in attendance to keep it running.

The important thing is that it works, and it demonstrates that the paper assessment of the feasibility study can actually be realised.

It is here that the key issues of principle are tackled, at least at the basic level. The assumptions of the feasibility study are tested against technical possibility. This phase needs creativity, strong motivation, a high level of technical expertise and a flexible approach to the way it is run. Too rigid a formal structure at this stage is usually counter productive. Often it will be necessary to change tack with regard to a particular problem.

Unless the project is so big as to make it impossible, the team for this phase should be kept fairly small – say a maximum of six or eight. Often, two or three are sufficient.

Responsibilities for specific aspects of the project can and should be assigned to particular individuals. But it is rarely possible at this stage to divide the project into clearly defined units to be worked on in isolation. Usually, all the aspects interact.

Many different ideas need to be exchanged, developed and tested in a very short space of time. This is best done in an informal environment. A particular team member may be leading the investigation into a particular issue at one moment, and providing advice and support to someone else the next. A rigid hierarchy gets in the way of this. In fact, the only structure which is really necessary is the existence of a project leader responsible for steering the project, arbitrating where necessary, and making sure that the goal is ultimately reached.

Output
The key output of the laboratory model phase is a working model. There should be a report detailing what has been learnt in building it but the formal specification will not have been significantly advanced by this phase. What has been gained is knowledge which will help in the design of the real system.

The user interface
One thing that can usefully be tried out at this stage is the way the product (or system, or whatever is being developed) is used. A working model of the 'user interface' allows experimentation with the number and type of knobs, buttons, switches and displays. This is an important part of the design, and it is

something that engineers do not always do very well. If you are familiar with what a product does, it is difficult to put yourself in the position of a user faced with something completely new.

Many good products have been spoilt by a poor user interface. Yet there is almost infinite scope in design, particularly in products that incorporate any kind of microprocessor.

Good design can make available to general users something that was previously restricted to technical experts. The car is a good historical example: early drivers had to be mechanics, and had to understand in detail how the engine worked in order to use it. Once the basic functions had been packaged, with simple and standard controls for starting, braking, steering etc, cars could be driven by anyone.

It is worthwhile to build a working model that is reasonably portable and can be tried out by the intended users. The results are often surprising. At the start of a project, some basic questions can be asked about how the product will operate. It is much more difficult to graft a new user interface on at a later stage. This is an area where marketing departments and end users can very usefully become involved. Often it is left to the engineers to define how the controls work – with the result that they work for engineers, and no-one else.

A further twist to this story is the realisation that there may be different types of users. If the end result of the development is a large piece of machinery, it is reasonable to ask how easy it will be for maintenance engineers to do their job, and how long the machine will need to be out of action while they do it. Modular replacement of parts is a good selling feature, but one that needs to be designed in from the start.

There is a well known saying in the computer industry: garbage in, garbage out. It applies to development projects too. The more precisely you specify exactly what you want from a development project, the better your chance of getting it. If you don't ask, the chances are you won't get it.

A laboratory model phase is not necessary in every project. If the technology is well known, and the method of operation well defined, there is no real need for a 'proof of principle' model.

Where it is needed is where new technology is being introduced for the first time, or technologies are being combined in a new way. The laboratory model is an opportunity to try things out at minimum risk and minimum cost. Once development starts in earnest, two things happen: the expenditure increases very quickly, and major course corrections become very difficult and very expensive.

DEVELOPMENT

The development phase is the real heart of the project, and where most of the money gets spent. The key issues of market requirements and technical feasibility should have been addressed. The important question now is not whether it can be done but How? How much? and How long?

During development, the team size can well expand by three or four times, and the expenditure will go up dramatically. At this point some projects begin to feel like a juggernaut starting to roll, and effective systems of organisation and control are needed.

Hopefully, previous phases have spied out the ground and drawn an adequate map. But a firm hand on the wheel, good brakes and good steering are essential. If the project leader has done his or her job well, motivation should not be a problem. The main difficulty is to avoid careering out of control.

The best approach is to build up speed gradually, and try out the controls until you have the hang of them. But the situation is more basic than that: you have to build the vehicle first before you can drive it. That includes putting in the controls you think you need and making sure they work. Many project leaders have found themselves halfway down the motorway before they realise that they haven't got a steering wheel.

Early in development, a detailed project plan is needed. An outline plan may well have been produced earlier for the purpose of estimating cost, timescales and resources. As development proceeds this can be revised and fleshed out. Planning is the single most helpful technique in establishing control over any project: it is discussed in detail in Chapter 4.

Building a good project team takes time. It is unwise to create, say, a 30-man team from scratch in one go. Sometimes, you have to do it, but it may be some time before the project is really under control. If at all possible, people should be brought in to the project only when they are needed, when there is a real job for them to do.

What is needed at the start of the development phase is a small team (again, six to eight is a good maximum size, and fewer is better) to lay the foundations of the design.

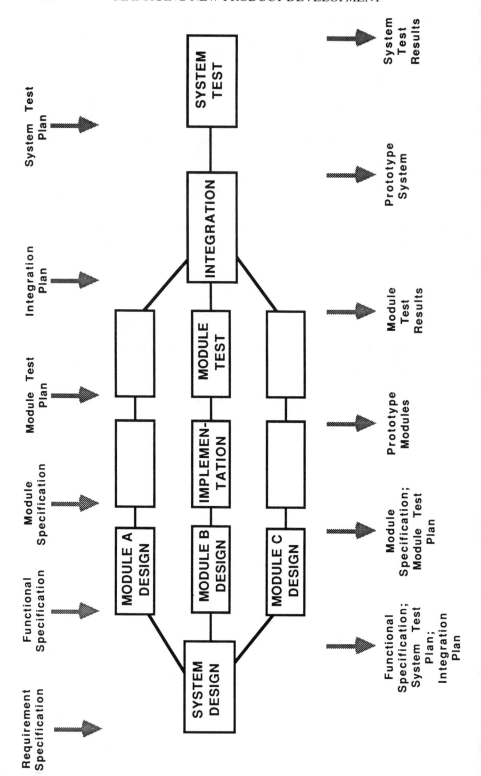

System design

It is useful to split the development phase into a number of sub-phases, each of which has its own characteristics (Fig 2.2).

The first, and in many ways the most important, task is system design. Any product, process or service can be regarded as a system of interacting parts. It is essential to analyse what these parts are and how they will interact before embarking on implementation. This avoids two problems: that the first idea that comes along is not always the best solution; and that different individuals will invariably seize on different and incompatible ideas if they are given a chance. It is vital that everyone on the project understands and agrees the approach to be taken before they start spending real money.

During system design the basic architecture of the system will be mapped out. Key decisions will be taken on how to implement the different requirements and these decisions will be recorded and communicated to everyone concerned. The feasibility study and laboratory model phases have acted as a trial run; this time the design is for real, and it must be right. Mistakes at this stage are very expensive. Something like 80 per cent of the key implementation decisions will be made here, and they will be difficult to reverse.

One of the most important jobs of system design is splitting the overall task into workable sub-tasks which can be assigned to different individuals or teams. Usually, but not always, the sub-project teams will correspond to some natural division of the final project or system. A team may be given a specific item of machinery to develop, or, say, be assigned responsibility for the electronics of the system. However it is done, the division needs to be clear. Overlapping responsibilities cause endless problems further down the road.

Module design

Once the system design has been agreed, detailed design of each of the sub-tasks or modules can go ahead. There is little point starting this before the system issues have been decided, except to research specific points that have a bearing on the system. There is always a temptation to start straight away on detailed design work. Resist it: rushing into implementation means either that work will have to be done again, or that the project will be forced down a road that leads to problems later.

Module design is simply system design on a smaller scale. Usually, the module designer will have participated in the system design, and he or she will go on to lead the module implementation team. On a small project, of course, he or she may *be* the implementation team (but still need advice or assistance from others on key technical issues).

During module design, the module designer may start to involve additional team members to help in deciding key issues, and will initiate them into the purpose of the project and the decisions already taken. Growing the team in this natural way allows relationships to develop and helps team members to understand and appreciate their role in the project.

Implementation

Module designs, when complete, should be reviewed by the system designer to ensure they fit into the overall scheme for the project. Once this has been done, implementation can begin. At this stage, the team should reach its maximum size. The corollary is that it also becomes most difficult to control.

Success here depends on how well the groundwork has been done. If the system design is solid, and module design well thought out, then each member of the project team should be clear about what they have to do. If the planning has been done well, they should also be clear about *when* they have to do it.

The project leader's role here becomes largely one of progress chasing and problem solving. A project, by definition, is not a routine activity. It will involve doing something that hasn't been done before. It is never plain sailing. The project leader's job should be to look for and anticipate problems before they become serious, and to solve them. Problems may come from any quarter and may require solutions that have never been tried before.

Integration

Modules developed separately must eventually be put together. This is the acid test of system design and interface specifications. But putting together things that don't work individually is a nightmare that should not be visited on anyone. Integration is the stage at which many projects founder. There are several reasons for this: one of them is trying to do too many things at once.

Modules should be thoroughly tested in isolation before

attempting to put them together. This may require developing a special 'test harness' that looks like the rest of the system, but can be manipulated step by step to see whether the module lives up to its specification. This is extra work, but it is worth it. I have seen projects spend months wrestling with complex problems built up of several simple errors. Usually the only solution is to pull the system apart and get the pieces working separately before trying to put them together again.

Integration should be done step by step. One interface at a time is plenty. Again, this may require special test harnesses, but it is well worth it.

Integration almost always takes longer than you think – sometimes many times longer. All the problems that have not been thought of, and all the misunderstandings and misinterpretations come out of the metalwork and laugh at the project team. If integration goes well, it is a tremendous boost to the project. If it goes badly, morale can be seriously affected.

The real solution lies earlier in the project: in attention to detail at the system design stage, and thorough specification of interfaces. Without benefit of a time machine, the best answer is a methodical approach which identifies the problems and tackles them one by one. This may involve drawing back and rescheduling integration for a later date. The relief when it finally works is keenly felt.

Test

System test is a final and thorough check that the system meets the needs set out in the requirement specification. It is important to step back from the problems of implementation, review what the requirement specification said and design a test to check it. Sometimes concentration on the detail causes temporary blindness to a serious system fault. It is often worthwhile to have a system test carried out, or reviewed, by someone outside the project.

If all is well, the system can be delivered. However, the end of this phase is rarely just a working prototype. What is really wanted, and is needed by the next phase, is a full documentation package. During system test, the opportunity should be taken to update and fill any gaps in the documentation. This is much easier to do while the information is fresh and while the project team is still intact and (hopefully) flushed with success.

The above is an overview which gives a flavour of the

development task. Many of the issues touched on here are taken further in the following chapters.

PRODUCTION ENGINEERING

In a product development, the development phase is usually followed by production engineering. Development proves that the product can be made once; production engineering ensures it can be made in hundreds, or thousands, or hundreds of thousands, and that it will survive for the expected lifetime of the product in the conditions for which it is designed.

Conventional wisdom is that you usually spend as much on production engineering as you do on development. While this can easily be true, it does not have to be the case. The traditional approach to product development has been to make it work, then worry about how you're going to make it (and about how much it's going to cost). There is an alternative. By feeding in a requirement for design-to-cost and design-for-production at an early stage of the project, many of the manufacturing problems can be identified and ironed out during development. This doesn't remove the need for a production engineering phase, but it does make it easier and very much quicker.

The kind of problems tackled in production engineering are:

- ease of manufacture
- cost of components
- cost of assembly
- test procedures and equipment
- manufacturing documentation
- component procurement
- environmental effects (temperature, humidity etc)
- robustness
- reliability
- safety
- regulations
- packaging
  etc

More than any other phase, production engineering requires a methodical approach and total attention to detail. This is a phase which benefits from a different type of skill, and from extensive practical experience of manufacturing problems.

Traditionally, the way to provide these different skills has been to hand the project over to a completely different team of production engineers. However, it is difficult to hand over all the knowledge and experience gained in previous work, and it takes a long time for the new team to become fully conversant with the project.

Traditionally, also, production engineers in the UK have been regarded as less skilled and less valuable than R&D specialists. This is hard to justify, and is definitely not so in other countries – in Japan, for instance, production engineering skills are highly prized.

A better solution in almost every way is not to regard production engineering as a separate activity, but as an essential part of the project throughout. Production engineering activity reaches a peak in this phase but it can be considered even during the feasibility study, where manufacturing issues should be high on the list of factors affecting the success of the product.

The requirements specification should set clear targets for product cost; the functional specification should consider how the product is going to be made as well as how it will work. Production engineering expertise can and should be made accessible throughout the development phase, to give views and suggestions on different implementation options. This approach is increasingly being adopted by companies around the world to reduce development time and stay competitive.

What happens at the end of development, then, is not a replacement of team A by team B, but a change in team composition. Some team members may drop out (or be available on call) as their work is completed; new members will be brought in with specific production expertise to boost the skills in this area. Activity will concentrate on proving the design in the real world as well as in the laboratory, and ensuring that it is cheap and easy to make.

Projects and companies both benefit if production engineers are regarded not as second class citizens, but as professionals with a vital expertise to bring to development. The cash flow of every manufacturing company depends crucially on production engineering skills and experience.

There are some projects where production engineering of the type described above does not play a part. Software does not require production engineering of this nature. It does, however, need to be engineered in another sense. It should be robust and give sensible results whatever use it is put to. A one-off project, such as a new company accounts system, does not need to be produced in quantity. It should, however, be reliable. And it should be easy to change as the company grows or alters and its requirements change.

Such projects do not have a production engineering phase. But there is a need for a post-development review, carried out in a methodical fashion, and preferably by an independent person, of fitness-for-purpose. This might be called 'usability engineering'.

PRODUCTION

For a product that is to be made in quantity, the handover to production is very much easier and quicker if a representative of the manufacturing site has been involved in the project during the production engineering phase. If the manufacture is to be subcontracted, this means starting negotiations during development. It may be necessary to adapt aspects of the design to conform to the manufacturer's build standards or available test equipment. There are often hiccups due to the different standards of documentation adopted by the developer and the manufacturer; sometimes a trial run is useful.

At handover to production, the product must be buildable (and testable) from the documentation alone. Those who will take on the documentation can be assumed to have a standard set of technical skills, but no special knowledge of the project. This level of documentation takes a long time to build up from scratch. It is much easier if the documentation has been gradually produced as development proceeds.

A product may go through several different versions on its way to manufacture, as the problems are gradually ironed out. The output of the development phase is usually a set of engineering models; during production engineering, alpha models (or A-models), and perhaps beta models, are produced. The pre-production run, in reasonable quantity and designed to test out the manufacturing procedures as well as the product, is often called a zero series. Pre-production units are often used for final trials, or for publicity purposes. Finally, units are produced to the full production standard.

TRIALS

Before making a product in tens of thousands, or before letting, for example, a new accounts system go 'live', it is sensible to expose it to a closed group of friendly users in a controlled way. Field trials (sometimes known as 'beta tests') often identify glaring errors missed by the development team, simply because they never thought anyone would use it that way. Habit is a major enemy in development, and habit can obscure what happens if you try to do something just slightly different.

Trials cost time and money, but they are always worthwhile. Recall of faulty products is not only embarrassing, it is very expensive. Some well known companies are rumoured to use their first thousand customers for field trials. Only do this if you have a strong stomach and can afford to risk losing your customer base.

LAUNCH

The end result of all this is usually the launch – of a new product, a new process, system or service. This is the time to count the cost, gauge the reaction and plan what's next. Good projects are satisfying (and frustrating, and exhausting, and hard work). Bad projects are all of this, without the satisfaction.

Commercial success depends on many factors, including what the competition does. A well run project, however, has its own satisfaction that comes from working as a team and achieving the objectives set. A project that succeeds is a boost to everyone involved and a springboard to better things.

3 SETTING THE GOAL

PROJECTS

A project is something set up to achieve a specific goal within a limited period of time. It is not a routine activity, and it is not a permanent organisational fixture. It will compete for resources and for management attention with all the other, well established activities of the company. It will probably cut across the normal management structure. Organisations which are willing to tolerate and support this will operate successful projects.

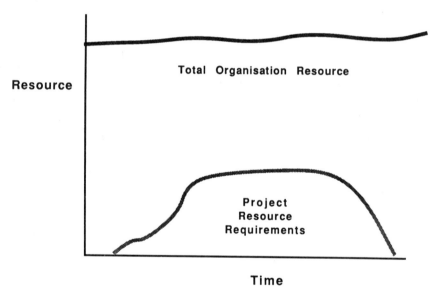

Figure 3.1 Project resource

Fig 3.1 shows the typical resource requirements of a project. Most organisations maintain a relatively flat resource level. There are small peaks and troughs as people leave and are replaced, and very occasionally a permanent step increase or decrease. The requirements of a project are uncompromising: to build up from zero to a peak over a relatively short time, and then to fall away again at the end, often quite steeply.

A small team may be built up early on to carry out a feasibility study and perhaps build a laboratory model. A larger team will then be required for full scale development and production engineering. These people must either be brought in from outside, or they must be reallocated from elsewhere within the organisation. This is bound to be an awkward process, and requires some difficult management decisions.

A common approach to project management in the past has been to appoint coordinators who will oversee activities relating to the project in different areas of the organisation. Contributors to the project do not work directly together, but hold committee meetings at intervals to compare notes. The focus of activity might start in the research and development department, then cross the boundary to manufacturing, and finally become the province of marketing and sales. Decision making happens through the normal departmental channels of the business, and responsibility passes from hand to hand as the project progresses.

This approach minimises disruption to the organisation, but at the expense of flexibility, cost and, above all, timescale. In order to *reduce* development time and improve efficiency, an increasing number of organisations have found it necessary to adopt a different tactic: one which gives direct responsibility to a project leader and a team to carry the project through from conception to launch. This approach to project management relies on a multidisciplinary team where the lines of authority and control are short. All the necessary information should be immediately to hand, and the skills directly available to implement key decisions quickly.

Rather than a linear succession of phases, often with a hiatus of several weeks during the handover period, it is possible to plan some overlap of activities to minimise the overall time (Fig 3.2). This can only be done because all the relevant skills are available in the same team, and the needs of production engineering (for example) can be considered early on in development.

Organisations which adopt this technique have found that it works, and that it dramatically reduces time to market for new developments. It requires the commitment to put development high on the priority list, and to organise to support it.

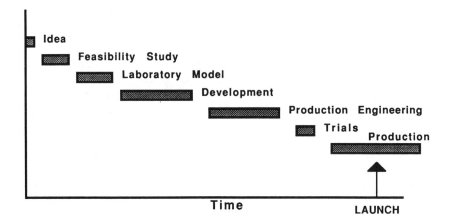

Traditional   Approach

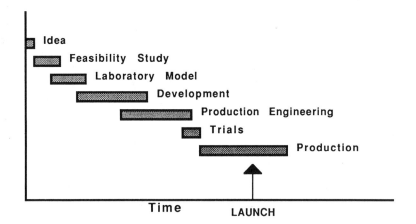

Competitive   Approach

Figure 3.2 Phase overlap

THE PROJECT LEADER

A project will not happen of itself. It is a departure from routine, and it needs to be driven. Always, the default condition is failure.

It follows that a project must be strongly led. Project leaders need both vision and drive: vision to see what is needed, and drive to make it happen. A project leader is not just an administrator. To achieve success, he or she needs to be given responsibility for achievement and the delegated authority to see it through.

A project needs to be championed at all levels of management. Issues raised often need to be tackled at the most senior level. It sometimes helps to appoint a senior person within the organisation (with the title, perhaps, of project director) to liaise between the project leader and senior management. This is a dual role: to help the project leader in making clear any special needs, and to watch over the project so that any major problems can be identified and resolved early. It can work well, provided the respective roles are clearly defined.

A project that is expected to bring in significant new business needs to be taken seriously, and should have corresponding exposure at the top level of management. This not only helps to motivate the project team, it provides the organisation with a clear view of progress and problems. It is also valuable feedback to the project.

The senior management of a company is usually in the best position to understand future markets and competition, and can give invaluable help in tuning the project requirements to best meet the future needs of the business. The main task of company management is, naturally, present business. But it is worth devoting a measured proportion of time and effort to building for the future.

This does not mean that senior management should take over the project. A project personally run by the managing director is a mixed blessing. The project certainly gets full attention and support, but a senior manager, unless he or she has given up all other responsibilities, rarely has time to devote the attention needed to keep a complex project running smoothly. A deputy, on the other hand, may feel reluctant to make decisions that could be overturned.

On any but the smallest project a full time leader is needed who has the responsibility and the authority to make key decisions. Some decisions, of course, have to be referred upward. The project leader should have regular access to senior management to explain what is happening on the project and to request support where necessary.

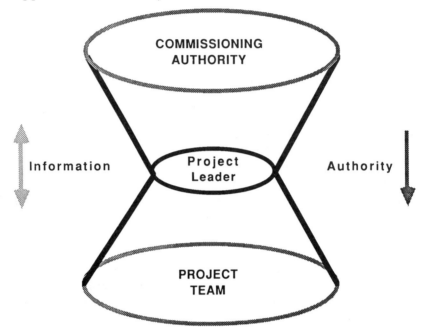

Figure 3.3 Role of the project leader

Fig 3.3 expresses the relationship between commissioning authority, project leader and project team. This single point focus for authority and responsibility plays a major part in bringing order out of development chaos.

DECISION MAKING

The first few weeks of any project are the most critical time. More decisions are taken than at any other time. Alternative lines of exploration are closed off, and the project is focused in a particular direction.

Unfortunately, decisions at this stage are often made unconsciously, or by default. This is partly decision overload – *something* has to be decided, and there is no time to waste. It is usually worthwhile to delay final decisions until rather more is known.

The phased approach is one way in which the decision load is spread. Decisions are taken in a controlled way – first on feasibility, then on design approach, and finally on implementation – as the relevant information becomes known. There is a second chance at phase boundaries to change decisions that have not worked out. The laboratory model phase is a way of having a first stab at a solution without all the constraints of the final product (cost, size etc). This establishes the basic knowledge from which the real decisions on technical approach and implementation can be made with confidence.

This phased approach to decision making does not mean delaying the project; rather, it means avoiding false starts, and not heading at full speed into blind alleys. By isolating key decisions and making them one by one at the appropriate time, each is given the attention it deserves.

In fact, all the techniques of development are designed to address the basic problem that an enormous number of decisions have to be made in a short space of time. A key skill of project management is in knowing which decisions to make when, and in having the relevant facts to hand when a decision needs to be made.

DEFINING THE NEED

The first question to be brought into the open asks what exactly is required from the project. *Not* making this clear is probably the single biggest cause of failure in all development work.

There are two ways in which lack of attention to the requirements can cause trouble. First, if the market or the user's real needs are not properly understood a great deal of expense and effort may be put into developing a technical success that will be a commercial failure. There are some famous examples of projects which have suffered this fate.

Second, if everyone involved in a project does not have a clear view of the goal, there is a serious risk they will head off in different directions. A surprising number of projects set out without a good definition of what is wanted. Worse still, everyone involved has a clear picture of what it is but the pictures do not coincide.

Anyone assigned to a project should take as their first task to identify the need, and to agree a clear objective that will satisfy it.

Identifying the real need is sometimes a delicate task. In order to do an effective job, a project leader needs to understand not only what, but why. Sometimes he or she will be given a detailed description of what is required. More often than not there will only be a vague statement, which needs to be investigated and defined precisely. Sometimes further investigation of what is asked for reveals an inherent contradiction. Often, there is only partial agreement among those commissioning the project as to what is really wanted.

The way to solve these and many other problems is to write and agree a requirement specification. This is the first, and arguably the most important, piece of documentation that should emerge from any project. It need not be lengthy. But its effect in avoiding misunderstandings is dramatic.

A requirement specification should, of course, be distilled from a great deal of information and discussion. It should contain the essential facts. But it is also important to understand the motivation.

The project leader should be aware of the background to the development, and should know where to go to clarify details which may not be written down. In short, the project leader needs to build up a close working relationship with whoever is commissioning the project, to back up the written instruction.

A cautionary tale
Too often the process happens rather like this:

- The project starts in a hurry, with a vague (unwritten) description of what is wanted.
- Some aspects prove technically difficult, and are dropped or modified without notice to those commissioning the project.
- Someone in, say, the marketing department has a good idea about a new feature and talks directly to a team member – bypassing the project leader. The likely impact on cost, timescale etc is never discussed.
- The product, when it is developed, meets with no-one's approval, because it is an undiscussed, unmanaged compromise. It is also late and overspent due to unexpected changes from all quarters which have not been properly planned.

THE REQUIREMENT SPECIFICATION

Two things are wrong in this potted history: communication and authority. But the situation can be avoided, given an understanding of what *should* happen. First, a specification should be written, on the basis of input from all who have a valid contribution. The specification should be discussed, agreed, and circulated to all.

Any changes during development should be suggested to the project leader. He or she will discuss and agree them with the appropriate people, then reissue and recirculate the specification. The specification is simply an unambiguous record of what has been agreed. Who has the formal authority to change the specification is something that each organisation can resolve. It could be the project leader alone, or the project leader in combination with a higher authority. Whatever the decision process, there is a written record which at any particular time is the final word on the agreed goal of the project.

The requirement specification is where market needs and technical possibilities meet. There is an art to writing one. It should be unambiguous, but comprehensible to both users and technologists. It should not, therefore, use technical terms unless these are unavoidable. It should specify *what* is wanted, but not *how* it should be done. Defining 'how' begs too many questions, and places technologists in a straitjacket which may be counter productive.

A requirement specification should be written on the basis of a full understanding of the market and a good appreciation of the technology. A market survey is very valuable at this stage. Certainly, the best marketing expertise available should be used in drafting the specification.

A good requirement specification should answer the key questions about the use of what is being developed – questions which are often forgotten. What should it weigh? How big should it be? Does it have to be portable? How much should it cost? These crucial points are sometimes left out in the race to define the technical content.

A suggested format for a requirement specification is given in Appendix E. The example is for a product development; for development of a system, or a piece of software, there are different considerations. However, many of the same categories apply.

GOAL SETTING

To be focused and effective, a project needs a concrete goal. The best goal is one which captures the imagination. The team which developed the Sony D-50 portable compact disc player was given a block of wood the size of a compact disc jacket and an inch and a half thick – about one twentieth the size of Sony's original CD player. This was to be the size of the new player.

Naturally, it was regarded as completely unrealistic at first. The project leader was not to be moved, however, and signed the block of wood so that it could not be changed. Design breakthroughs were required, as well as the setting aside of preconceived notions on how CD players should be constructed. The goal was achieved.

Setting a goal, of course, requires judgement. Sony only succeeded because they had the resources to develop new semiconductor devices and precision assemblies to do the job. The major achievement, in this and many other cases, lies in breaking the mind set of 'It can't be done'. This will not happen without a clear and challenging goal.

MANAGING CHANGE

Writing something down does not fix it irretrievably. It simply makes it clearly visible. The ideal is a concrete goal and a written specification that remain solid throughout the project. This is rarely achieved.

In the real world, requirements do not stand still. Markets change, and new competitive products are announced that dictate a change in strategy. Further technical knowledge may suggest new features, or indicate that what was originally asked for is not technically possible or economic. It usually falls to the project leader to manage the process of specification change.

Changes in the specification always disrupt the project, and invariably cost both time and money. A problem with many projects is that such changes, or 'creeping enhancements', are accepted without allowing additional time, cost or resource to implement them. The result is that the project overspends, and is late. It is up to the project leader to evaluate and indicate the effect of any proposed change. This acts as a natural deterrent to change for change's sake. Of course, the project leader cannot produce a convincing evaluation without an adequate project plan and a budget.

An agreed procedure for changing the requirement specification solves a lot of problems. This may involve a meeting between the project leader and key representatives from senior management, marketing or whoever has commissioned the project. It does not pay to make changing the requirements too easy.

ROLES

After *what*, the next most important question is *who*. Put the right people in the right roles and the project (will almost) run itself. This needs to be done at the start, because it is difficult to correct later.

The first two tasks to be assigned in any project are project leadership and system design. In some cases, the project leader may carry out the system design task. But on a large project there is usually enough to do in planning, coordinating activities, solving resource problems and managing the relationship with the commissioning authority. A separate system designer is usually required to look at the key technical issues of the product as a whole. The system designer should be brought on board early in the project (preferably during the feasibility study), and where possible should carry the project through to completion.

Projects work best if there is a clear division of responsibilities between team members. They also work best if individuals can do their jobs with the minimum of interaction. A project is prevented from being an exercise in 'design by committee' by giving each person an individual design task which adds up to a well defined and carefully coordinated whole.

During feasibility study and laboratory model phases, design tasks can be assigned as the need arises. The development phase, however, needs a more formal structure if it is to run smoothly. The appropriate project structure should start to become clear as the system design progresses. While the design for the product is being crystallised, the project leader should be working on a design for the project team.

It often helps to build the project team around the structure of the product. A competent system design will identify each component part of the system, and specify its interaction with other components. This forms the basis of a design task which can be given to an individual or a sub-project team.

PRODUCT ISSUES

The system designer will view what is being developed as a collection of interacting parts. But, particularly where the end result is intended for mass production, it is helpful if there is someone on the project who takes a different view: that the end result is a single entity (in many cases a physical box) conforming to certain basic constraints.

This person will be responsible for issues such as the final cost of the product, its basic construction, its safety, how it will be tested and so on. Early on, the role may be simply to act as an advisor. In the later stages, these product engineering issues will assume more and more importance, and will dominate in the production engineering phase (Fig 3.4). This approach eases the transition from development to production, and helps to reduce overall development time.

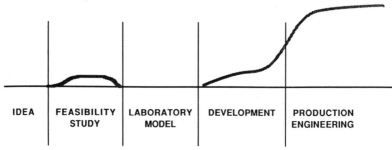

Figure 3.4 Product engineering involvement

On a small project, the three key roles of project leader, system designer and product engineer may be carried out by one person. With a larger team, it becomes necessary to split out the roles to ensure that each of them gets adequate attention. Fig 3.5 shows appropriate structures for small (up to eight people) and larger (20+) projects.

SINGLE POINT RESPONSIBILITY

Ultimately, an activity will only happen if someone is responsible for making it happen. This simple truth extends to all levels in a project.

The first step is for someone to be responsible for the project as a whole. Many projects drift into existence with no one being sure exactly who is in charge: there may be two or three candidates. It is vital to resolve the question of who is running the project from the word go. Team members need to know who to communicate their problems to and who has the last word in resolving disputes or problems. Someone needs to be responsible for seeing what is *not* being done, and fixing it.

If there are several candidates for project leader, all with valuable contributions to make, then it is possible to create

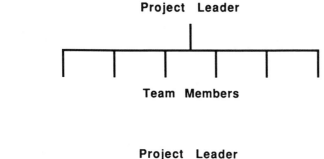

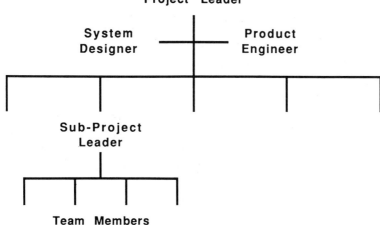

Figure 3.5 Project structures

additional roles for them: perhaps as project supervisor, or reviewer, or system designer. If this is done, the breakdown of roles and responsibilities should be made very clear to everyone. What is essential is a single individual who has the power (and is seen to have the power) to make clear decisions about the day to day running of the project. Checks and balances, advisors and reviewers, can be added, and the balance of power can be tuned if it is not working. If necessary, a project leader can be replaced – perhaps by switching roles with someone else. But the central role must remain, and must be clear to all. Experience shows that, quite simply, other structures do not work.

The need for single point responsibility extends from the project leader through to every task in the project. Unless it is absolutely clear who is responsible for a task or a component or a function, the chances are that it won't get done. Problems will be left for someone else to solve. Resolve this, and it can make an immediate difference to attitudes and to results.

Most people react well to responsibility – at the appropriate level. Lack of responsibility is one of the commonest causes of frustration among capable people, and frustration is highly damaging in any team activity. Paradoxically, however, few people will actively seek it out. Responsibility is satisfying, but it is not comfortable. It falls to the project leader to make absolutely clear who is responsible for what, and to reinforce the point whenever necessary.

A project leader can disrupt single point responsibility by bypassing the authority of whoever has been assigned to a task. This is damaging, and should be avoided except in an emergency. The right solution is to work with the team member who *is* responsible, offering guidance where necessary; or explicitly to reassign responsibility.

A good manager understands the personal aims and capabilities of his or her team, and will assign responsibilities accordingly. Usually, the best results come from stretching individuals just a little beyond what they feel comfortable with. Of course, you cannot just do this and walk away. Some form of supervision by a more experienced person is necessary. This need not be formal or take too much time, but it should be there.

Ultimately, many of the problems of development come down to the issue of responsibility. If it is not possible to point to any part of a project and state immediately which individual is responsible for it, there is likely to be a problem, latent if not actual. A project without a clear structure is unmanageable.

DEPARTMENT VERSUS FUNCTION

Many development organisations are structured according to engineering discipline: an electronics department, a mechanical engineering department, a software department and so on. This helps to build expertise and exchange ideas in each discipline, but it can cause problems when it comes to a project. Loyalty is built up to the department rather than the project, and creating a team spirit can be hard work. Project teams usually return to their own departments to work, creating communication problems. This type of structure leads to the standard arguments over development problems ('It's the fault of the electronics.' 'No, it must be the software ...'). It is difficult to establish single point responsibility in a departmental structure.

Much better from the project point of view is a multidisciplinary project team built around the functions required of the product or system. Wherever possible, teams should sit and work together. Lines of communication and control are kept short, and problems can be nipped in the bud. Team members may have specific skills, but their responsibilities are built round the needs of the project. Gaps do not occur.

Once they have adapted to this way of working, team members usually find it more productive and satisfying. Individuals in this type of organisation are much more in control of their own destiny, and rely less on others to solve problems for them. Real goals can be set and results achieved in place of excuses.

This is a cultural wrench to some organisations, but it works. The departmental structure can be retained as a backdrop, with department heads coordinating the assignment of resource to projects, ensuring standards are maintained, training new recruits, and determining career progression. But for successful development in the minimum time, the project structure needs to be emphasised and supported as the primary means of getting things done.

STATUS AND ROLE

In most of the activities of business, senior status (in terms of career development, peer perception and remuneration) usually translates into a senior role in the organisation. Development, however, is not so simple. Development activity is a mixture of skills, both technical and management. Different projects need different sets of skills at different points in the project hierarchy. If it is always necessary to allocate the 'top' jobs in a project to people with the highest status, development activity will be severely constrained.

Project hierarchy, in any case, is a rather misleading concept. Sometimes the key to an entire project is solving a specific technical problem in one small area. This may be the most crucial role in the entire project, but sits somewhere near the bottom of the hierarchy.

The only way to solve this may be to appoint a very senior person to deal with the problem. It is not necessarily appropriate that they take over the whole project. If the organisation culture allows senior people to work for and take directions from juniors, within the context of a project, then development problems will be very much easier to solve.

It follows that there has to be some other means of determining status rather than the current, temporary, role in a particular project. Some organisations have a 'technical ladder', progress up which depends on the accumulation of past work and overall contribution to the organisation. This can also solve the problem of development engineers who do not want to become managers, which is the standard route to career progression in all other business activities. In some organisations, promotion means losing valuable technical skills, and creating some very bad managers.

The technical ladder is a good approach. It needs a great deal of organisational will to maintain it, since the mental pressure to conform to standard business practice (status = role, seniority means management) is very strong.

MOTIVATION

The best development work is done by a team that enjoys working together to meet a collective challenge. A development team is a diverse collection of creative specialists. Each is driven by different private goals, but there are some common denominators to motivation:

- Excitement
- Responsibility
- Challenge
- Teamwork
- New experience
- Career development.

Development requires attention, concentration and creativity. Straightforward pressure works up to a point, but too much pressure on a development team can be counter-productive, leading to mistakes and frustration. An enthusiastic team, on the other hand, will work through the night to complete a task. The best type of pressure is the challenge to meet a particular deadline – perhaps a demonstration to a client or a senior manager – built on a foundation of real enthusiasm for the project.

Excitement is motivating. The excitement may be technical: 'This is something new and ingenious that no one has ever done before'. Development organisations usually have their own culture, which is often a separate sub-culture of the organisation. In some development cultures, technical excitement is the only type of enthusiasm that is accepted. It is a useful asset; but it can also lead a project into strange byways that may have nothing to do with the real goal.

There is a more productive type of enthusiasm: one that includes meeting the real needs of users. This is something that is particularly well appreciated in Japanese organisations. In some cultures – particularly if there is a 'them and us' feeling between engineers and management – it simply would not be understood.

Developing such an attitude relies on engineers knowing what the real need is. In some cases, no one has ever taken the trouble to explain to them what customers, or end users, really do with the product that is being developed. This is always a worthwhile investment.

In some places, an attitude survives that the role of the designer is to tell the customer what he really wants. Such an attitude is damaging to the health of the project, and of the company. It can be changed, but it needs to be done by example and cannot be done overnight.

Building the right kind of motivation comes from understanding the personal goals and interests of team members. In development, 'brute force' motivation – money, for example – does have an effect, but it is limited. Good development engineers can usually command a high salary wherever they go. They are likely to place a great deal of emphasis on job satisfaction and career development. Factors such as salary and working conditions have two effects: they may persuade an engineer to join a company if the conditions are right, and will encourage him or her to look elsewhere if they are not. But they will probably have little impact on the quality of contribution to an individual project. This is more likely to depend on personal enthusiasm for the project, the attitude of the project leader, and working relationships with the project team.

Most engineers are enthusiastic about a new project provided it is presented well. Keeping enthusiasm alive for the whole distance is more difficult. Inevitably, there will be low points. Positive results, like an early working model, are a good motivator, as are team spirit and good working relationships.

Communication helps: team members often feel in the dark about how the project as a whole is progressing, what is happening in other areas, and whether there is any feedback from senior management, marketing or potential users. The project leader, who has access to all this information, can easily assume that it is finding its way to the project team. It won't, unless he or she takes steps to communicate it. Semi-social occasions, such as project lunches, are a good investment: they encourage the exchange of ideas and information and help build working relationships.

Team members should feel that their work is being noticed. This is particularly important where a project team is seconded from other parts of the organisation. A project team is an impermanent structure which offers little direct opportunity for career enhancement. The project leader should make sure that the department leaders concerned know about the work their people are doing, and will take account of it when they return.

Responsibility itself, of course, is a good motivator. Boredom breeds dissatisfaction; challenge creates enthusiasm.

4 SEEING IN THE DARK: THE NEED TO PLAN

WHY PLAN?

If you drive better with a blindfold, don't plan. If you can do without a steering wheel, even better. Ordinary mortals, however, will find that planning is both the clearest means of forward visibility, and the most effective way to steer a project in the right direction.

Planning on a small scale is a natural ability that we all depend on for our survival. Planning a project is something that needs to be learnt and developed. The effort required to do this is well worthwhile, since it transforms a project leader's ability to make effective decisions and to make them stick.

Many people do not produce a plan, and justify this for one of the following reasons:

- It takes too long – we need to get on and do the work
- I don't need it: it's all in my head
- Planning is for planners, not doers
- Plans are never up to date
- It doesn't work, anyway: my projects are still late.

Of those who do, many do it under sufferance ('The rules say we have to have a plan; let's get it over with so we can get down to the real work').

This is a pity, because of all the techniques available to the project leader, planning is the one which will gain the most benefit for the least effort. For senior management, a plan is also the best means of assessing the progress of a particular project, and seeing what problems lie ahead.

To be effective, however, plans must be used. Frequently, a

great deal of effort is put into drawing up a detailed plan at the start of the project. The plan then sits on the wall or lies mouldering in a desk drawer, becoming increasingly irrelevant as the project changes around it. Plans need to be updated. Plans should lead to actions, too. Frequently, all that a plan is used for is to record just how late the project is getting. It is no wonder that many project leaders regard plans, and planners, with suspicion.

The greatest benefit of planning is that it can identify problems in advance, before they have a serious impact. More than that, it can suggest how problems can be resolved and show the likely outcome of different strategies.

PLANNING TOOLS

Many people's attitudes to planning have been shaped by the tools and techniques which were available five to 10 years ago. Planning used to be a complex and time-consuming task, often requiring a staff of specialist planners who were remote from the real project work. Planning tools based on large computers (or, worse, manual methods) were difficult to use, and the time between feeding a new set of information to the planners and getting a useful result could be several days. Separate drawing office resource was often needed to draw up the results into useful charts. In these circumstances, much determination was needed to use plans effectively. And, of course, considerable investment was required to keep the whole exercise going.

Modern planning tools, based on microcomputers, have transformed the situation. Inexpensive and powerful microcomputers, together with new software planning packages, have made the most sophisticated techiques directly available to the project leader in a simple and accessible form. The latest planning packages have graphical interfaces so that project plans can be drawn directly on the computer screen. Using these tools, a moderately complex plan can be updated in about half an hour, and the results seen immediately. 'What if' calculations (What if this piece of equipment arrives late? What if this activity takes two weeks longer? What if I assign some more resource to this part of the project, and take it away from somewhere else?) can be done in minutes. Plans can actually be used, rather than seen as a necessary (or unnecessary) evil. These facilities are available within the budget even of small companies.

The tools exist, but tools alone are not enough. Simply buying a software package will not resolve anyone's planning problems. Project leaders need to know how to use plans, and must want to use them. In the end this comes from experience, and from seeing concrete results. This chapter sets out the basics of planning: how to create a plan and how to use it effectively. It is a start; the rest, inevitably, is up to the reader.

PLANNING TECHNIQUES

There are several different planning techniques, and almost as many names for variants on the same basic method. For development use, there are two important types: bar charts (Gantt charts, etc) and logic networks (PERT, critical path analysis, etc).

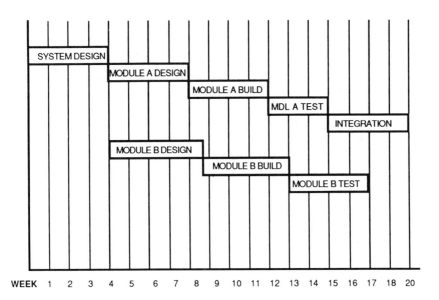

Figure 4.1 Bar chart

Bar charts are widely used. Usually drawn on a scaled time axis, they show the duration and position in time of each activity (Fig 4.1). They can also be used to show when a particular person or resource is needed on the project. However, they do not show the logical dependency of one activity on another. There may be hidden problems in Fig 4.1: for example, can integration really start before Module B Test is complete? They are difficult to update if anything slips or advances: the whole chart usually needs to be redrawn. However, bar charts are easier to handle manually, which probably accounts for their widespread use.

Networks show, in addition to time, how the different activities depend on each other. In Fig 4.2, the boxes represent activities; the lines show logical dependencies. TEST cannot start until both BUILD and PRODUCE TEST PLAN are complete. The numbers written above each box are the earliest start date for that activity, and its duration in working days. Although time still flows from left to right, networks are not usually drawn on a scaled time axis. (However, most network planning packages will automatically produce scaled bar charts when required.)

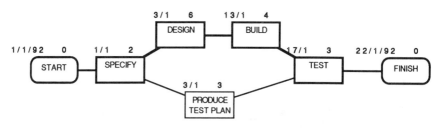

Figure 4.2 Logic network

Networks also show the *critical path* through a project. In Fig 4.2, DESIGN and BUILD together take 10 days, while PRODUCE TEST PLAN takes three. The test plan can be written at any time during the 10-day design and build period. If it starts a day late, or takes two days longer, it will not affect the overall time taken. However, any delay in SPECIFY, DESIGN, BUILD or TEST will delay the whole project.

This chain of events (shown in bold) is the critical path: it is the longest sequence of activities on the project, and will determine the overall timescale. It makes sense for the project leader to concentrate on the activities of the critical path, and even transfer resource from other, non-critical activities to cut down the overall project time. Fig 4.2 is a very simple plan: on a real project the critical path can take some quite surprising routes.

Knowing the critical path (and the next most critical, and the next) is key information that is difficult to get other than by drawing a logic network. It allows the project leader to focus attention on the most important activities. It is often possible to reduce the overall project time (and cost) by reassigning activities and resources.

It may appear that networks are more complicated and more difficult to comprehend than simple bar charts. To use bar charts effectively, however, you need to be aware of all the links and logical dependencies between tasks. Once set up, a network will automatically handle these for you. It requires a little initial effort to understand how networks operate and to use them to the full, but it is well worthwhile.

The only real disadvantage of logic networks is that a computer-based planning package is needed to use them effectively. Networks can be calculated manually, but it really isn't worth the effort. Both microcomputers and planning packages are now so inexpensive compared with resource costs that a planning package can easily pay for itself several times over on a single project, in effort and time saved. Several planning packages are available to run on standard general purpose microcomputers, such as the Apple Macintosh or the IBM PC.

NETWORK NOTATION

In the remainder of this chapter, I shall concentrate on planning using network techniques. To complicate the picture, two types of notation are commonly used. Fig 4.2 is an example of an *activity-on-node* diagram: the boxes (or nodes) represent activities, which take time; they are joined by arrows, which are simply logical connections and take no time at all. Fig 4.3 is the same plan in *activity-on-arrow* notation. This time the arrows represent the activities. There is little to choose between the two notations; I have used activity-on-node diagrams throughout this chapter for consistency.

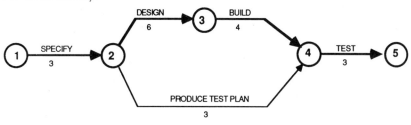

Figure 4.3 Activity-on-arrow network

Fig 4.2 and the other activity-on-node diagrams in this chapter were produced by the MacProject planning package, running on an Apple Macintosh microcomputer.

CREATING A PLAN

There are two very distinct tasks in planning: creating the plan, and using it. During the creation stage, a model of the project is being built up. Once this has been done, the model can be used to assess progress, anticipate problems and try out strategies for resolving difficulties.

Creating a plan is a useful exercise in itself. It allows everyone to get clear in their minds exactly what needs to be done, what depends on what, and what problems there are likely to be. In creating the plan, you are setting the pattern for the project. The decisions taken at this stage (consciously or unconsciously), the assumptions made, and the explicit or implicit commitments given by team members, will play a large part in determining the future course of events.

Producing a plan does have its pitfalls. Technical folklore is full of stories about the beautiful and elegant plan that bore no relation to reality, the plan that overran by 200 per cent, or the plan that missed out three crucial activities. Many of the pitfalls can be avoided by following a few simple rules. The steps required to build a plan are decribed later; below are some general points to bear in mind while drawing up a plan.

Clarify the goal

If the goal isn't clear, there is no point even starting to plan. Chapter 3 describes the process of goal setting in some detail.

Involve the people

Develop the plan together with the people who are likely to work on it. Apart from giving a more accurate result, this starts to involve the team, gets them thinking what will be required, and is a first step towards commitment.

Imposing a plan without consultation can be counter-productive. For a team member who takes pride in his or her work, there are few things worse than being presented with someone else's detailed plan of how to do your job, and being told to get on with it. Some people take it as a personal insult. Others are sorely tempted to prove the plan wrong. Anyone, however, who is asked to venture an opinion on how to do something is already involved, and on the road towards commitment. Even if the opinion is clearly wrong, it is a starting point for discussion and a good opportunity for the project leader to communicate what really needs doing.

This is best done by gentle leading, rather than bulldozing. There is rarely time to bulldoze everyone on a project. Project teams are far easier to manage if individuals are self-motivated.

Delusion and optimism

It is wise to forget all about timing and resources until the *logic* of the plan has been established – that is, a description of all the tasks with the interconnections between them.

One of the classic traps of planning is self-delusion. This is often manifested as working backwards: 'The project has to be finished by this date, therefore this part will take this long'. It is easy to justify missing out an activity, or cutting a few days off a timescale, by a mental gymnastic along the lines of 'We have to do it, therefore we'll find a way'. This, unfortunately, does not work. Good intentions, freely made, tend to evaporate in the heat of development.

Utopian plans may be comforting, but they are worthless. Reality is much harder to manipulate than a plan. An accurate plan can help bring reality into line, but a false plan simply puts off the day of reckoning, while problems fester unobserved in the darkness.

The best way to deal with the temptation of time pressure is simply to remove it. Draw up the plan initially as an answer to the question 'What will it take to achieve this result?' – *without* any constraints of time. Then add the timings.

Similarly, the initial assumption should be that there is always adequate resource. Resource constraints can be put in later; the logic of the plan should show what activities *could* be done in parallel. This gives maximum scope later on, when it may be worthwhile, say, to double the resource on an activity that is on the critical path, in order to shorten the overall project time.

Divide and rule

For a large project, it is useful to split the task down into areas of activity to make the planning task more manageable. Inevitably, there will be interdependencies. But it is easier to take one area at a time and resolve the interdependencies later than to draw a single large plan that tries to encompass everything. This also makes the plan easier to read.

Figs 4.4a and 4.4b show two methods of dividing a plan up in

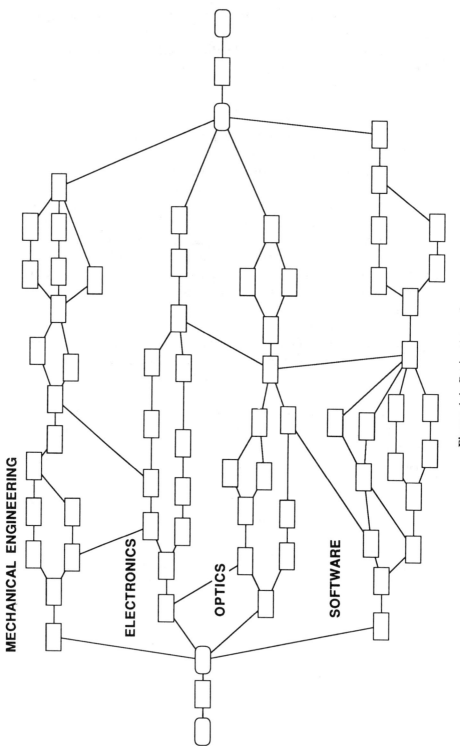

MECHANICAL ENGINEERING

ELECTRONICS

OPTICS

SOFTWARE

Figure 4.4a Project 'strata'

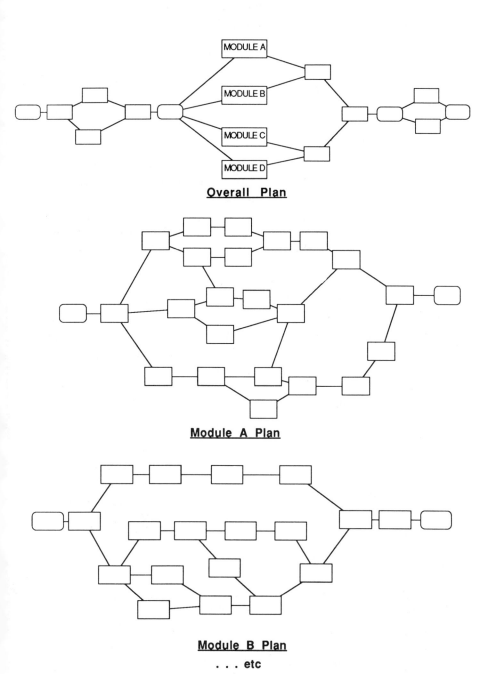

Overall Plan

Module A Plan

Module B Plan

. . . etc

Figure 4.4b Sub-project plans

this way. In Fig 4.4a, the plan is divided into horizontal strata representing different responsiblities – electronics, software, optics, mechanical engineering, etc. The division need not be completely rigid, but it is a convenient way to make the overall task more manageable. In Fig 4.4b, separate sub-plans are drawn for each sub-project module. In this case modules are likely to be interdisciplinary, with each sub-plan covering a wide range of skills.

Which is most appropriate depends on the project and on what is being developed. Small projects or ones where the activities are closely interdependent are probably best tackled by the strata method. If the project is large, or if it splits naturally into independent modules with little interaction, the sub-project method is better. In this case there are likely to be a number of sub-project leaders, each of whom is responsible for one of the sub-plans.

Difficulties arise if the project is large *and* the activities are closely interdependent. If the plan turns out to be very complex, with cross links in all directions, this may be an indication that more thought needs to be put into the structure and organisation of the project. If the plan is difficult to manage, then the project itself will be more so. It is worth asking whether the project can be rethought to divide it into smaller sub-tasks that can be tackled relatively independently. (See Chapter 3, 'Roles'.)

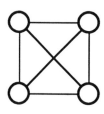 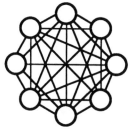

Figure 4.5a Growth in communication paths with project size

Fig 4.5a shows how, as a project team grows, the number of possible interactions between team members grows too – roughly as the square of team size. Beyond a certain size the situation becomes uncontrollable and there is no alternative but to split into smaller units with clear interfaces between them (Fig 4.5b). This may not be easy, but the alternative is chaos. This is simply good system design, and it applies to project teams just as much as it does to products.

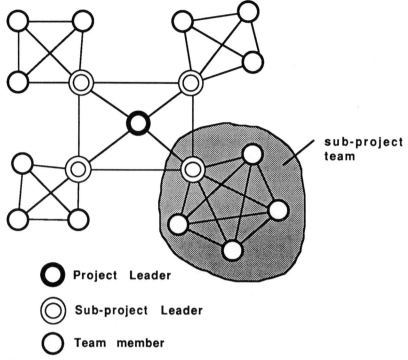

Figure 4.5b Project structure makes large projects manageable

The naming of tasks ...

A key skill in planning is choosing what is important and deciding the right scale of task to put on the plan. A plan that lists every single activity in detail will be enormous, and probably of no practical benefit. A plan that misses out key activities, on the other hand, is at best misleading. A planner needs to identify the important tasks – those that will give clear signals as to how the project is going.

For example, should an electronics development task be entered as BUILD PCB, or broken down into LAY OUT PCB, PROCURE PCB, 'procure components' and ASSEMBLE PCB (Fig 4.6)? The answer will depend on a number of things, including the project leader's confidence in the people carrying out the work. If past experience shows that this always happens like clockwork, it is not worth labouring the point. On the other hand if there is a risk of delay in, say, procuring the components, or of PCB layout taking twice as long as it needs to, then it is worthwhile drawing out the detail so that each individual task can be progressed. Extra detail increases visibility of the project and the degree of control, but complicates the plan.

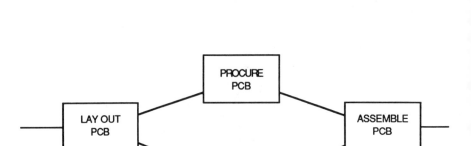

Figure 4.6 Plan alternatives

Dependencies also affect the way tasks are defined. If just one part of a task is dependent on some other activity, then it is probably necessary to separate out that part as a separate task, so that the logical dependencies can be drawn correctly.

Whatever the task chosen, it should have a definite and demonstrable end point which is not capable of misinterpretation. 'Continue design' is not a good task description: when can it be said to be complete? The naming of tasks is a neglected art form, in which project leaders need to become expert. A good task description should convey, in very few words, a positive action that has a definite completion point. It should also sum up all that needs to be done. 'Complete' is a good verb to use: 'complete design', 'complete testing' etc. 'Begin' is dangerous, although it is sometimes necessary. 'Continue' should be avoided.

The typical length of a task will vary, depending on the size and type of the project. A long task is difficult to check up on. The only way to assess progress is to make a judgement such as '50 per cent complete', which is very difficult to do. Tasks have a tendency to stick at '90 per cent complete' for a surprisingly long time. It is far better, for morale as well as project control, if task sizes are chosen so there is a reasonable chance of completing one or more tasks between each update of the plan. As a general rule of thumb, a small number of working days is a good task size for a detailed plan.

PLANNING IN PRACTICE

The best way to illustrate how a plan is built up is by an example. Suppose that, for a particular industrial process, the pressure inside a chamber must follow a particular pre-set pattern as the process develops. The profile depends on time, and also on the conditions of the process (including temperature). At present, this is all controlled manually. A computer-controlled vacuum pump is wanted that will provide the required pressure at each stage automatically.

This is a project which involves mechanical engineering, electronics and software. We will assume that some sort of requirements specification exists as the result of a previous feasibility study, and that a laboratory model has proved the viability of the control techniques proposed. What remains is the development phase.

The first step in the plan is to look at the product as a whole and determine how the different elements will be put together. For the moment, this system design activity can be represented as a single box on the plan, although it may be useful to come back and expand it out later. As a result of system design, a functional specification should be produced detailing the key decisions taken and the interfaces between different parts of the system.

Before going any further it is sensible to review the system design, since the decisions taken here will be difficult to reverse.

So far, then, the plan looks like this:

Figure 4.7 The first three stages

The START box is drawn with rounded corners because it is not an activity but a key event. The next box after Fig 4.7 will also be a key event: SYSTEM DESIGN COMPLETE. We can regard this as a milestone – a point of significant achievement which is worth highlighting on the plan. So far, there are no dates or durations: the plan simply records what has to be done.

Up to now, the system has been considered as a whole. However, if SYSTEM DESIGN has done its job, it will now be

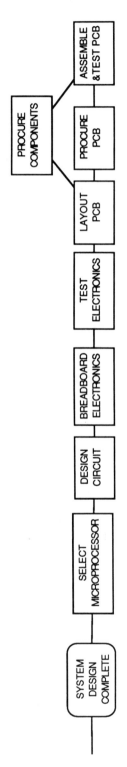

Figure 4.8 The electronics stratum

possible to split the development into parallel sub tasks, with an engineer or a small team assigned to each. Until the system design has been done, it is not strictly possible to identify exactly what these subtasks will be. For the purpose of planning, though, we can make a reasonable judgement which can be refined later. As this is a small project, we will assume that the overall task will be divided along discipline lines: mechanics, electronics and software.

Electronics

Taking the electronics stratum first, it might look like Fig 4.8. The electronic circuit will be designed around a microprocessor. This needs to have inputs from pressure and other sensors, and from the keys and switches on the control panel; and outputs to the pump, control valves, alarm signals and, probably, a control panel display.

The first task is to select the microprocessor. This is brought out as an activity on its own, partly because it is important in itself, and partly because some of the software activities will depend on it (as we shall see in a moment). Factors which might affect the choice of microprocessor are the speed at which things need to happen; the type of calculations which need to be done; and the hardware and software support available for different types of microprocessor. The question should have been raised, and may have been resolved, during system design; but in practice there are often some loose ends like this which need more detailed research to provide an answer. Although this task is written in the 'electronics' area of the plan, software engineers will obviously need to be consulted in the decision process.

Having taken this basic decision, circuit design can proceed. For those not familiar with electronics, a 'breadboard' is the first test build of a circuit using wire wrap or other quick assembly techniques. (I hesitate to say a 'lash up', because it is possible to produce a reasonably professional breadboard.) Breadboards are often used for a first circuit test, because it can take several weeks to produce a proper printed circuit board (PCB).

Having tested the breadboard, PCB layout can start. It is not explicitly stated on the plan, but it is assumed that any problems with the breadboard circuit are corrected before going to PCB. The PCB test should be simply a matter of checking that the layout and PCB manufacture have been done correctly, and that the circuit still performs as it did on the breadboard.

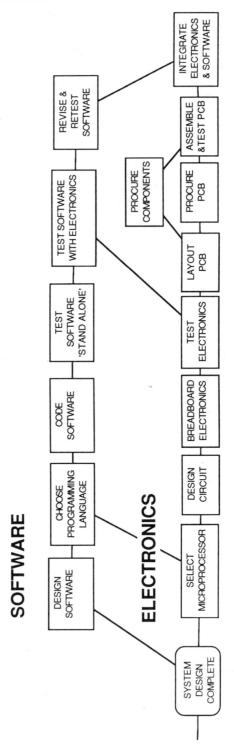

Figure 4.9 The software stratum

Component procurement is a task that should not be forgotten. Where one-off circuits are being built, it is not usually a problem. If the intention is to build 50 prototypes, or if there are any non-standard components, then it can become a major headache. Procurement lead times can be surprisingly long, and can fluctuate wildly according to semiconductor supply and demand. Many projects have reached a crucial stage only to be held up for one or two components which have not been ordered, and are on eight or 10 weeks lead time.

Any problems found on the PCB when it is tested are likely to be fixed by 'cut and strap' techniques: cutting copper tracks and soldering new wires to make connections where necessary. Another PCB version will be made later in the project to tidy up this kind of modification.

Software

The software stratum of the plan might look like Fig 4.9.

Software design is the activity many people miss out, in their desire to get on with actual programming. This is a mistake. Trying to write a program without first establishing the basic architecture is rather like designing a mechanical component at the milling machine.

A 'stand-alone' test of both software and electronics hardware is important before trying to integrate the two. Otherwise, the possible combination of faults is a real nightmare. One of the cliches of development is that software engineers always blame the hardware and hardware engineers blame the software. Project leaders often have to referee.

The link between TEST ELECTRONICS and TEST SOFTWARE WITH ELECTRONICS reflects the obvious fact that software cannot be tested on the electronics until the electronics is ready: obvious, but sometimes forgotten in scheduling. (In Macproject, the direction of links is always *from* the activity at the left end of the link *to* the activity at the right end of the link. On manual diagrams, arrows are often used to show direction.)

It is assumed that the testing will reveal some problems, and there is an explicit activity to revise and retest the software. The final box is an integration test, which should go through all the functions required of the system and check that they operate correctly with the final versions of PCB and software.

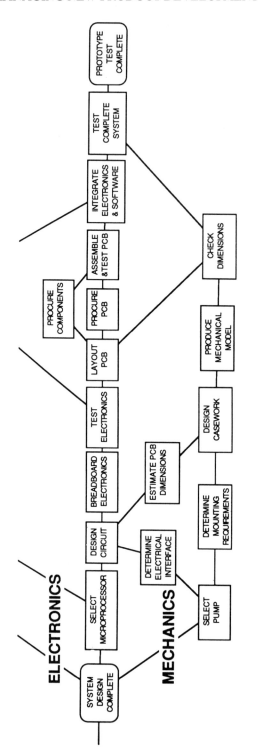

Figure 4.10 The mechanics stratum

Mechanics

The mechanical engineering task in this case is relatively simple (Fig 4.10). It consists of selecting an appropriate pump (assumed to be a bought-in item), and making sure that the complete product is suitably cased and mounted. Since this is an industrial product, we will assume that its visual appearance is not of overriding importance. If this were a consumer item, considerable effort would be spent early on in concept sketches and model making, to ensure that the product looks good and will appeal to the chosen market.

Having selected the pump, details of the electrical interface required must be passed to the electronic designers. The pump mountings, and the mechanical interface to the process chamber, must be determined. But before the casework can be designed, a good estimate of the size and shape of the PCB(s) must be obtained from the electronic designers, together with requirements for cooling and airflow, etc. Position and nature of the display panel must be confirmed.

Mechanical design can now go ahead, with mechanical drawings and a prototype assembly. But as soon as a real PCB is available, the actual dimensions should be checked – together with component heights and mounting points. It is not unknown for PCBs to be changed in the heat of the moment without informing the mechanical designers. Often it is the simple things that cause the problems. It has been said that in any electronics development, two things always go wrong: the power supply doesn't work, and it won't fit in the case.

Checking the logic

So far all of this is on paper, and the only thing that says the project will happen as planned is the intention of the project leader and of the development team. It is wise for anyone producing a plan to show it again at this stage to the key people on the development team and ask them to check it. If the development team is determined to go another way – or if the plan is simply wrong – it is scarcely worth the bother of printing it out.

Development requires commitment and creative effort, and forcing people to work to a plan they do not believe in is not the way to get it. Sometimes it is necessary to do it and build up commitment later. But climbing the north face of the Eiger is that much more difficult if the team feel that they really should have taken the west route rather than the east. Far better if this is all sorted out at base camp. In development terms, this means thoroughly checking – and communicating – the fundamentals of the plan before you start.

Estimating

Having drawn out the logic, the next job is to add time and resources. The job specification for this exercise lists patience, determination, and a degree of diplomacy among the key requirements.

When tackling a routine task, or something that has been done several times before, it is easy to arrive at a realistic estimate. Unfortunately, many development tasks consist of things which have not been done before. They may be done by people who are not known to the project leader. On a multidisciplinary project, several of the tasks may involve skills that the project leader is not personally familiar with. How do you arrive at reasonable estimates, and set realistic goals?

In this situation, the prime source of information has to be the people who are doing the work. Patient questioning is usually the best approach to finding out what activities are required. Stupidity, whether feigned or real, is sometimes useful in clarifying exactly what needs to be done, and what depends on what. Many people are used to doing things instinctively, and do not analyse exactly what steps they go through. Often, it is only in trying to describe it precisely to someone else that the process becomes clear.

The only real basis on which estimates can be made is a comparison with previous tasks. The classical approach to estimating is to keep breaking a task down into subtasks until you arrive at something you can compare with known activities. This really works, and can produce accurate results – as long as you eventually arrive at a set of subtasks that are familiar and documented. If the task is completely new, however, estimates will always be approximate. Whatever the situation, estimates are always worth making in order to set a goal, and ensure that a better estimate can be made next time.

Like plans, estimates are far more valuable if they are done together with the person concerned. An agreed estimate contains an element of personal pride; an imposed estimate invites rejection. Recriminations after a critical goal has been missed are of little use to the project.

Some people are reluctant to give any estimate at all. Giving a figure represents an element of commitment. A volunteered figure is far more valuable than anything suggested by the project leader.

Project leaders should not take estimates at face value. Some people consistently estimate too high to give themselves room to manoeuvre. Many people estimate too low, often because they can see the major activities clearly but do not allow enough time for subsidiary tasks, integration, problem solving etc. It is worth investing some time in assisting team members to improve their estimating skills.

If you do not agree with what has been suggested, you should continue the discussion until both participants can agree and commit to a particular figure. This is far better than either walking away with a figure that you don't believe, or imposing something that the other person does not accept. In both of these cases, the project is likely to lose out.

The project leader needs to record, mentally, the degree of confidence he or she associates with each estimate. This is a complex judgement that cannot easily be fed into a plan, but it should be borne in mind when reading and interpreting results.

For the purpose of calculating overall timescale and critical path, what is important is the *elapsed time* that a task will take. This is usually measured in working days or working weeks. Many planning packages allow task resourcing to be indicated as well (for example, five days of a designer, one day of a draughtsman, and two days of a technician). This is very useful for resource loading and cost calculations, but the important figure for critical path timings is the overall task time – perhaps seven days in this case.

Goals

Estimating is not simply a passive task of making a guess and then waiting to see how it turns out. The estimating process should be the basis for setting realistic goals, which are agreed with the individuals concerned. Once this is done, all concerned can work on the common task of ensuring that the goals are met.

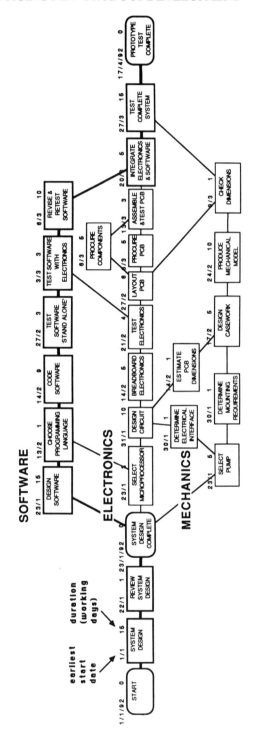

Figure 4.11 The complete plan with critical path

THE CRITICAL PATH

Fig 4.11 shows the complete plan with task durations added. In fact, each activity is shown with two figures: the earliest start date, and the duration (in working days). The earliest start date is the first date at which it is possible to start work on the task – that is, when all activities on which the task depends have been completed.

Fig 4.11 also shows the critical path (in bold). This is a strong indication of which tasks need special attention as the project progresses. It also shows the end date: assuming a start date of 1 January 1992, prototype testing will be complete on 17 April. This is actually the *earliest* date at which the project can be completed, and assumes in particular that none of the tasks on the critical path is delayed.

Most planning packages allow a variety of dates to be displayed, such as earliest start, earliest finish, latest start, latest finish. Earliest start and duration are usually the most important figures.

Another key quantity relating to each task is the *float*. This is the number of days by which a task can be delayed before it affects the overall project. If any task is delayed or extended by the amount of its float, it will automatically become critical, and risk delaying the project. Float is a useful index of criticality, and a good guide to which tasks need the closest attention. All tasks on the critical path have a float of zero (unless the project is already late, in which case the float can be negative).

A common error in project management is to look at the float associated with a task and assume that all is well as long as the float is not exceeded. Unfortunately, as soon as the float is used up by a particular task, other tasks dependent on it will immediately become critical. Float is not available to be used separately by each task: it is shared. If all the float is used up early on, all later tasks must be completed within their allotted time or the project will be late.

Fig 4.12 illustrates this. Here, not only earliest start but also latest start dates are displayed (at the bottom left of the activity boxes). The latest start date is the latest date at which the activity can start without delaying the project. The difference between the earliest start and latest start dates is the float for that activity.

Look at DETERMINE MOUNTING REQUIREMENTS, the second activity in the 'Mechanics' section. This task has more

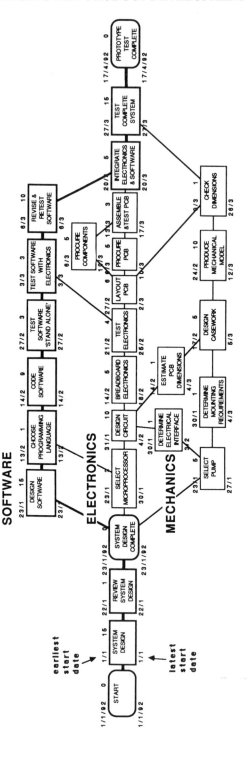

Figure 4.12 Earliest start and latest start

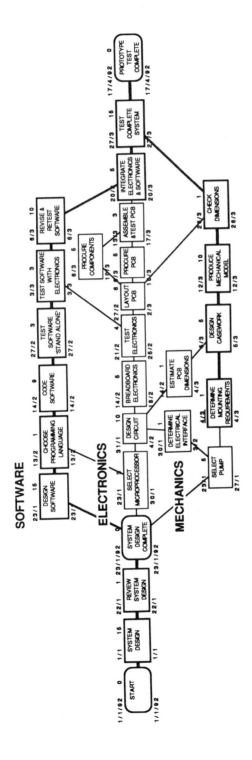

Figure 4.13 The effect of using up float

than a month of float. Although it can be done as soon as the pump is selected, say on 30/1, it does not have to be started until 4/3. The temptation is to leave it until it is actually needed. But this means all the subsequent tasks in the mechanical line become critical (Fig 4.13).

Fig 4.13 also shows that it is possible to have more than one critical path: this simply means that two paths in the plan take exactly the same time. It is also quite common for two paths to differ by only a day or two, which is why looking at *the* critical path is never quite enough.

All this explains why telling team members exactly how much float there is on their particular activities is not always a good idea. If everyone uses up 'their' float, the project is in trouble. What is really needed is to set an agreed goal for each activity, based on the float available and a degree of judgement.

Some planning packages will produce a 'float order listing', setting out all activities in order of float, with the most critical tasks at the top. This is useful in that it allows not just the critical path but the next most critical path, and the next, to be seen. It is worth tracing these out on the plan to understand how the dependencies arise. Sometimes, they are surprising.

RESOURCING

Resources can also be added to the plan. Packages differ in how they handle resourcing. Macproject allows up to six resources to be specified for each task. Fig 4.14 shows the plan with resources assigned to each task, from the following categories:

MECH	Mechanical engineer
ELEC	Electronics engineer
SW	Software engineer
TECH	Electronics technician
REVIEW	Review panel
DO	Drawing office

On a real project, it is best to use names rather than general categories: this brings home the point of responsibility for each activity.

Macproject will then produce a resource bar chart (Fig 4.15), showing when each resource will be required. Float is

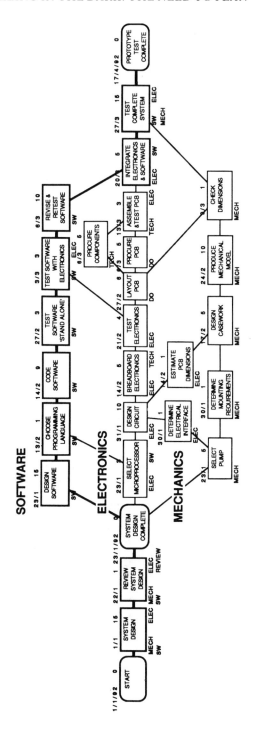

Figure 4.14 Plan with resources assigned to each task

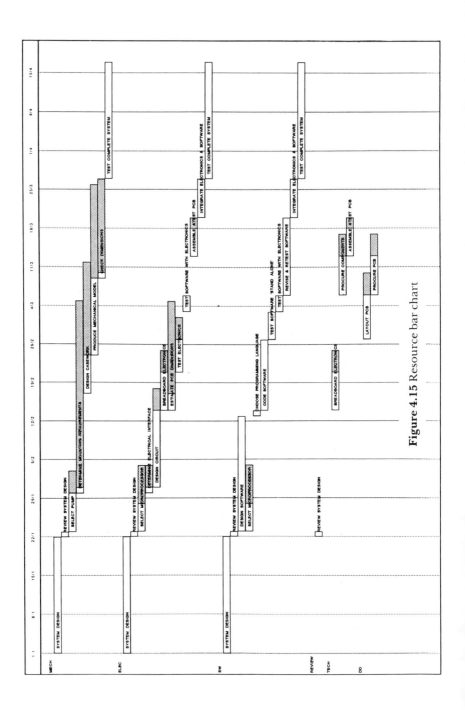

Figure 4.15 Resource bar chart

represented by the shaded areas. All tasks without shading are critical. Where one person is seen to be doing two tasks simultaneously, this may be cause for alarm – although the tasks may not require 100 per cent attention. It may be necessary to extend the timescale or put back the start date of some tasks to take account of the available resource. Some tasks originally drawn as parallel on the plan may need to be done sequentially, simply because the resource is not available.

Some packages, such as Microplanner, allow resource histograms to be produced, showing the percentage utilisation of each resource over time (Fig 4.16). If the resource is a single person (or a single piece of equipment), any requirement greater than 100 per cent is clearly going to be a problem. Tasks may need to be rescheduled. Depending on the amount of float available, this may or may not delay the project.

On a complex development project, histograms like this are very useful. They can identify workload clashes in advance while it is still possible to do something about them. If they are not provided automatically by the planning package, it is sometimes worthwhile to produce them manually.

A word of warning with regard to computerised resourcing: development staff usually have a unique mix of skills (and levels of skill). When working with a computer plan, there is a temptation to juggle resources and schedules until the numbers

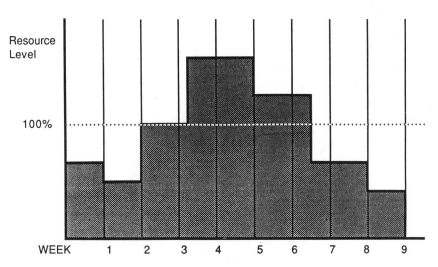

Figure 4.16 Resource histogram

fit on the screen or on the printout. This may work on, say, construction projects, but the application to development requires more care. Exchanging one person for another needs to be thought through with regard to type of skill, level of skill and degree of motivation. It will often be necessary to increase or decrease the time for a task, or to do things a different way.

WHAT IF...?

Up to now, a great deal of effort has been put into producing a computerised model of the project. Now, it can be used.

Fig 4.11 shows that the critical path runs through software development. This is not surprising, since the difficult part of this project is going to be developing the control algorithms required. But what if the electronics task has been underestimated? Suppose the only electronics resource available is a junior designer, who is likely to take twice as long to complete the circuit design?

The effect is easy to see. Simply change the duration of the DESIGN CIRCUIT task from 10 to 20 working days. Fig 4.17 shows the result.

The critical path has suddenly shifted to electronics. Surprisingly, though, the first critical task after the design review is selection of the pump – because this will determine the electrical interface to be designed into the electronics. The overall effect is to push the end date of the project out from 17 April to 29 April.

Looking at the plan, various options are available to reduce the delay. It might be possible to speed up the pump selection, perhaps by making a provisional choice to be confirmed later. Or electronics design might be started on other areas of the circuit with the pump interface being added later. Usually, something can be done: it is not necessary to accept the situation at face value.

SQUEEZING THE PLAN

Often, the first attempt at a plan comes up with an end date that is way beyond where the project leader and his or her employers would like it to be. It may be that the product will miss its market if

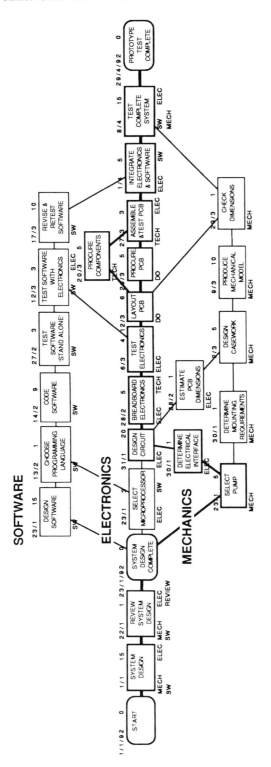

Figure 4.17 Shift of critical path to electronics

it really takes that long – or the company itself may even be at risk.

It is possible to do something about this. An experienced project leader can often take as much as a third out of the timescale of a first draft plan. This does not mean the plan is wrong. If it has been properly drawn up it should accurately represent how long the project will take, given the current organisation and resourcing and the level of risk that is presumed acceptable. The plan may even be optimistic, since it requires careful management to ensure that none of the tasks on the critical path slip.

The plan can be changed, but only by taking specific actions to change the assumptions on which it is drawn up. This requires commitment, and often some hard decisions. Simply changing the figures on the plan is not enough. Everyone involved has to (a) believe it is possible and (b) commit to achieving it.

Some improvement can usually be gained by shifting resources to tasks on the critical path, from activities where there is plenty of time. Beyond a certain point, the only way to make further improvements is to add resources from outside the project. There is also a limit to this: after a while, adding further manpower becomes counter productive. (This applies particularly to software; see Chapter 7, 'Team size'.)

A close knit organisation also improves things (see Chapter 5, 'Working Together'). This, however, may be a wrench to existing organisational structures. Motivation and commitment, naturally, helps. Time can be saved by taking calculated risks, although these need to be carefully defined and recovery strategies developed. A risk that the final product will not work correctly is probably not acceptable; the risk of concentrating on a particular design approach may be worth taking – perhaps with an insurance policy of looking in parallel at alternatives.

Some indication of the potential for improvement can be gained by looking at the plan. If there is a single critical path and many non-critical activities, then there is probably room for improvement by concentrating on critical path activities. If there are several parallel near-critical paths all vying for attention, then the plan may have been squeezed as much as it can be.

With the right level of commitment, from the organisation and from the people, remarkable results can be achieved. Without it, any plan is likely to slip.

WORKING WITH PLANS

Everything so far discussed can be done before the project starts in earnest. If planning stopped here, it would still be useful. But the real benefit is gained by using a plan in action.

The most common use for a plan is in monitoring progress. However, plans can do far more than this. In fact, slavishly following what was decided on at the start, simply because the plan says so, can do more harm than good. A plan should be flexible enough to allow changes of direction in a controlled way and for good reasons.

A plan should be a living model of the project, simplified enough so that it can be manipulated and different approaches tried out. When deep in development, it is sometimes hard to see the wood for the trees. It is the project leader's responsibility to take a longer view than the current number one problem. The greatest help in doing this is the plan. The plan will indicate when it makes sense to cut and run on a particular problem, and try a different approach. The plan will also show when there is likely to be a workload clash, because an activity has been delayed and the same person is going to be required for two things at the same time. The plan will point out when two groups of people will want to use the same piece of prototype equipment, and when it will be necessary to hire a special test kit to carry out a particular set of tests. It will also give an up to date, realistic estimate of when the project will finish, and suggest reasonable goals to set for particular milestones.

Updating
However, the plan will not do any of these things unless it is regularly updated. There is a two-way feedback between planning and the project itself. The plan predicts and sets goals; the project achieves particular results which are fed back into the plan and used to refine its predictions. Without this conscious feedback, planning loses touch with reality.

The frequency of updating the plan depends on the project. The project leader should be aware at all times of what is happening, particularly in the critical areas. But a formal update of the plan is best done at one go at intervals of, say, a week or a fortnight.

This means checking progress in every area, with the people who are actually doing the work. The questions to ask are:

- What tasks have been completed since the last update?
- How much time is still remaining on tasks which are under way?

This only takes a few minutes for each task but can often turn up problems, particularly in obscure corners of the project which may have been assumed to be progressing nicely because no one has raised a song and dance.

The success of updating relies partly on the fact that a single person has been assigned ultimate responsibility for each task. There is therefore, a unique and authoritative source whom the project leader can ask about each task, and to whom he or she can feed information on the progress of other related activities. The formal update (which need not be too formal, provided the key questions are answered) brings home the point of responsibility and makes sure that no areas of the project are being forgotten. Without this, it is all too easy for a project leader to become absorbed in a particularly pressing problem and not see the storm which is brewing just out of sight.

Having updated the plan, it should be communicated to the project team. Some project leaders distribute a copy of the complete plan; others send a list only of relevant tasks to each team member. It is important that each team member understands the goals they have to meet. It is also valuable for team members to understand how what they are doing fits into the overall scheme. Unless there is a good reason why not, everyone should at least have access to the full plan. The only point to guard against in doing this is that team members do not calculate the float on their task and take it as an indication of how much they can afford to slip. If problems of this nature arise they are best dealt with on a one-to-one basis, by explaining exactly what float means, and setting personal goals for the task concerned.

Course correction

The weekly (or fortnightly) update gives a 'snapshot' of the project at a particular time. The revised figures, when processed

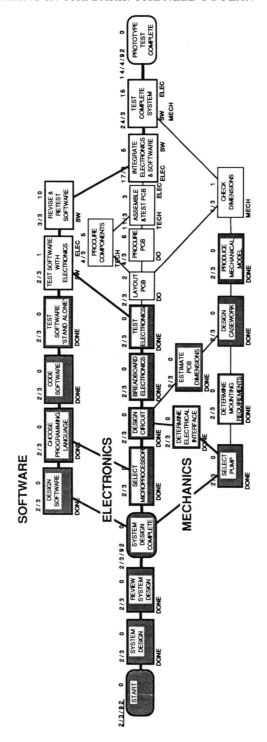

Figure 4.18 Two-month update

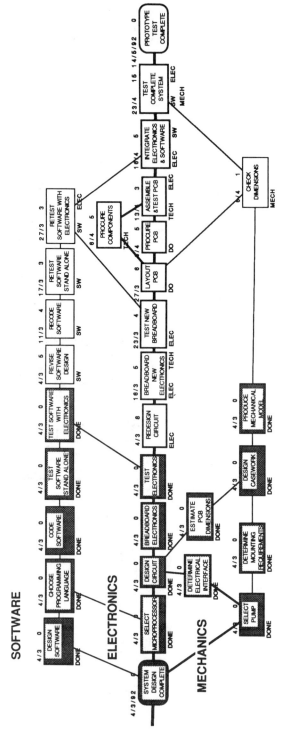

Figure 4.19 Plan showing likely delay of a month

on the computer, may well change the critical path and the projected end date. The project leader will often need to take some action to correct, say, a slip in a particular area, or a new resource clash that has arisen.

Take the plan produced earlier (Fig 4.11). Fig 4.18 shows the situation after two months have passed. There are various ways of updating a plan; the method used here is to set the task duration on all 'done' tasks to 0, and to set the START date to today's date. The plan will then reflect the current status. 'Done' tasks have also been shaded on the diagram.

Electronics development has taken two days longer than expected. Software, which is on the critical path, has gone well and is three days ahead of schedule. Fig 4.18 shows the position with one day remaining on the test of software with the electronics. The predicted end date has been brought forward three days.

However, as the tests continue a problem is found. To provide the necessary sensitivity of response to conditions in the process chamber, two extra sensors need to be fitted. This necessitates a significant change to the electronics and a rewriting of the software control algorithm. The effect is shown on Fig 4.19: a total delay of almost one month to the project.

Is there any way of reducing the delay? Suppose the prototype is to be demonstrated at a crucial exhibition, which will be missed if this delay stands?

Fig 4.20 shows a solution, arrived at after some discussion and replanning. The main change is to carry out much of the system test using the breadboard electronics, only substituting the PCB for a final week of testing. This is not an ideal solution, and it means that the breadboard must be designed to fit into the final mechanics, which was not necessary before. However, the extra effort and risk mean that it will be possible to meet the exhibition date.

This much effort, of course, is not always justified. If this was a sub-project that was not on the overall critical path it would be better to play safe, acknowledge the slip and use the plan simply to contain the problem. Where a special effort *is* justified, the plan shows exactly where to put it and how it can be controlled. In this case, the crucial dates for testing and negotiation will be closely monitored to ensure they are met.

In fact, it is never necessary to put concentrated effort on every area of a project. The plan will identify where extra effort

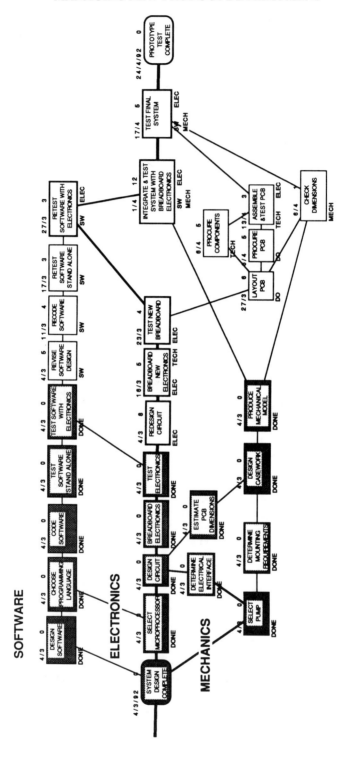

Figure 4.20 Plan showing solution to likely delay

can be applied to yield most benefit. If a project is late, the reaction of many project leaders is to put the whole project into panic mode. This is not only unnecessary, it is often counter-productive. A tired and demoralised team makes mistakes; work is often done twice, and done differently. Team members will rush to complete a particular task, only to find it is not going to be used until much later, and probably needs to be modified anyway. Different groups will be in conflict over access to equipment.

This way lies chaos and disaster. A plan can identify which tasks need to be done when, can spread the load among team members, and ensure nothing gets missed out. People will respond to a challenge provided they can see that their work is going to be useful. When a project is under pressure, the last thing which should be left out is planning.

5 ORGANISING FOR SUCCESS

A successful project needs organisational procedures that provide a strong backbone of control and support, without placing the whole enterprise in a straitjacket.

Organisation by itself is not enough: the best techniques in the world will not succeed if there is inadequate motivation, or responsibility is not delegated appropriately. But it is the small details of organisation and administration that either oil the wheels or bring the whole venture to a shuddering halt.

MEETINGS

Meetings are an excellent way to waste everyone's time. On the other hand, they can be very effective if used in the right way, and with a clear understanding of what you want to achieve. Some of the basic facts about meetings in a development context are set out below.

Size
The larger the meeting, the harder it is to get anything done. This is simple mathematics, and common sense experience. If you are trying to reach a decision, any group larger than six or eight is extremely hard work. Three to four is much better.

Participants
It is important to have the right people at a meeting. If you are trying to reach a decision, invite the people who are directly concerned. Don't exclude any of them, particularly if they hold opposing views. Don't include anyone who isn't really affected: this simply wastes time. If the right people are not available,

reschedule the meeting. If they don't turn up (or send a representative), you may have to decide without them – but tell them why.

Type
Meetings are called for different purposes. Some of the most common are listed below.

Decision
A meeting called to reach and agree a decision. Participants may have views beforehand, but should be open to discussion. The full facts may only emerge at the meeting.

Agreement
A meeting called to agree a decision already (partly) formulated. You need to present a case and have it accepted.

Information
A meeting called to pass information to attendees. This may be notification of decisions already taken, or it may simply be factual data.

Opinion
A meeting called to collect information and/or opinions from attendees.

Progress
A meeting called to assess progress against some plan, and set (as well as motivate towards) new goals.

Instruction
A meeting called to teach participants about a particular skill, or some aspect of the project.

Review
A thorough analysis of a particular aspect of the project, often done with expert assistance from outside the project team. On a large project, it is worthwhile to set up a regular review programme. Reviews of the whole project should be carried out at phase breakpoints.

Discussion
A meeting called to exchange views, with no particular aim.

Decision and progress meetings need to be small. With a larger group, the options are limited. On a large project, *staggered* progress meetings work well: individuals or small groups can be arranged to come in at, say, 15-minute intervals to talk about their area of the project. The discussion covers only progress, plans and problems; technical issues are noted down and separate meetings set up to cover them. Once participants (including the project leader) have been trained to keep to a timetable this system works very well, and avoids a large meeting of the whole project.

If a decision is required from a larger group, the best option is often to proceed as follows:

1. Hold an 'opinion' meeting to allow people to express their views
2. Formulate a proposal incorporating those views. Discuss it with one or two representative people (especially those with strong views)
3. Hold an 'agreement' meeting to agree the proposal.

All this, of course, takes time and is best avoided where possible. It can be used if a project is being carried out for a large group of people (say, the senior management of a company), all of whom want a say in the outcome. Wherever possible, though, a single representative or a smaller group should be appointed to represent the views of the larger body on a day to day basis. The justification is simply reduction in time, effort and uncertainty.

Inexperienced project leaders tend to hold a lot of discussion meetings. Discussion, however, is best done informally. A formal discussion meeting (ie a meeting with no specific aim) is rarely useful except as a social event: meetings should have a purpose.

Discussion meetings are, however, useful in one circumstance: where communication has not been taking place naturally. This can occur if there is a build up of misunderstanding, in which case a discussion will often clear the air. It can also occur if a development is taking place on two or more separate sites, in which case any way of promoting communication is a good thing.

Time
The timing of a meeting is not unimportant. Should a progress meeting be Friday afternoon or Monday morning? A Friday

meeting consolidates the week's work, and sows the seed for inspiration in the bath on Sunday; a Monday meeting wakes people up and sets clear goals for the week.

Most people are not at their most alert immediately after lunch. Some people are at their peak in the morning; others do their best work late at night. Setting a meeting at 8.30 or 5.00 makes an obvious statement.

Lunchtime meetings (with food) have an informal atmosphere, and can be useful for information and/or opinion meetings. Social or semi-social gatherings can be useful in promoting a team attitude and building trust. Project lunches, and the occasional project dinner, are worthwhile institutions and sometimes lead to useful cross-fertilisation. They will not solve the world's problems, however.

Attitudes to the scheduling of meetings will reflect the culture of the organisation, and individuals' status within it. In some companies, meetings are simply announced and people are expected to attend; in others people are asked what would be the most convenient time. Project leaders can follow the standard line, or they can deviate slightly from it: these things will be noticed by the project team.

Place

The location of a meeting does a great deal to set the tone. Meeting rooms should be reasonably quiet, and moderately (not overly) comfortable. Noisy and cramped meetings waste time and cause frustration. If there is a meeting room assigned to the project, meetings should be held there. Lack of adequate meeting facilities can cause tremendous frustration, and every effort should be made to resolve it.

Informal meetings can be just as important as formal ones – if not more so. Facilities can be designed to make informal meetings easy or hard. Some companies go out of their way to provide comfortable coffee areas where people can meet and talk informally. This encourages cross-fertilisation between projects and between disciplines. Many good ideas can be generated this way, in addition to the chat about the weather. (Free coffee, incidentally, has an effect on morale which is totally disproportionate to its cost.)

How to use meetings

Before you arrange a meeting, be clear why you want it. Sort out (and write down) the purpose. This will usually be one or more of the items on the list mentioned earlier. Consider carefully who to invite, and the size of the meeting. Choose an appropriate time and location. Chair the meeting (if it is your meeting). State the purpose at the start, and bring it back on course if it veers off. Set a time limit, and keep to it. Apologise if you or the meeting are late. Sum up at the end, state what has been decided (if appropriate), and clarify actions for the participants. All meetings should finish with an action list, specifying what, who and when. None of this has to be done formally, or stiffly.

People respond to a successful meeting. Decisions resolve uncertainty, which liberates the energy tied up in worrying. People really do go away refreshed after a good meeting. Bad meetings, on the other hand, sap energy and lead to frustration and depression. They are not inevitable: you can do something about it.

SPECIFICATIONS

What was said about the requirement specification in Chapter 3 applies at all levels of the project. Before embarking on a difficult development task, it is important to know just what is wanted.

The product described in the requirement specification will normally be split into a system of interconnecting modules for development. The specification for any particular module is, in effect, an agreement between the system designer and the module designer as to exactly what this module has to do. It saves a great deal of confusion and rework if this is written down.

Writing down the specification does not fix it for ever. It simply clarifies in the minds of everyone on the team what this part of the system will do. Once established, the specification becomes a natural mechanism for clarifying and communicating any changes.

Small, close-knit teams can do without specifications for a while. But the project usually comes unstuck when somebody leaves, or even when some time has elapsed since the original development and no one can remember why it was designed that way. Teams which are large, or dispersed, or where the members do not know each other well should always start by building a full set of specifications. This establishes channels of communication and working relationships as well as setting out the basic design. It is cheaper and quicker to correct mistakes on paper than in real life.

However, it is not always possible simply to write down a specification. Some experimental work may be needed to establish what is possible, or what is most economic. This can be done during the laboratory model phase or early in development. In fact, the level of experimentation necessary will determine whether a laboratory model phase is needed. Once the relevant experiments have been done, however, the decisions made should be committed to paper – and, where possible, reviewed (see below).

The requirement specification should be the first element in a 'tree' of specifications which gradually builds into the design for the final product (Fig 5.1). In general, the tree should build from the top downwards (since the trunk of this particular tree is at the top), although experimentation may be happening at all levels. Some detail of the design may be a key risk area that is crucial to the project, and may need special investigation to determine its feasibility early on. However, even here the final shape of the design will not be known until the specification tree grows out to meet it.

The first item to be produced after the requirement specification is a functional specification. The requirement specification answers the question 'What?'; the functional specification addresses 'How?'. A functional specification will typically contain:

- a system block diagram
- description of operation
- division of system into modules
- requirements for each module
- interfaces between modules
- interfaces to the outside world
- key technology issues/decisions
- environmental/safety/regulatory issues.

Appendix C gives a suggested format for a functional specification in checklist form.

All implementation issues which affect the whole system should be covered in the functional specification. A specification hierarchy should not contain any repetition, since two copies of the same thing always run the risk of getting out of step. Therefore it is sensible to treat environmental issues (for example) at this level.

The functional specification is also a sensible place to specify module interfaces, since it is the one common link between any two modules. Two separate descriptions of the two sides of an interface are quite likely to be inconsistent.

The functional specification can be a long document. It should become the 'bible' for module designers, covering all the key issues, at least in outline. If it becomes too large, it is worthwhile to separate out as sub-specifications those parts which are frequently changed – for example, a module interfaces specification. This minimises the amount of paper to be copied on re-issue.

Responsibility
Specifications are a natural way of clarifying the distribution of authority within a project, and of bringing home the message of single point responsibility. The author of a module specification is the one person responsible for that area of the project, and the one person who is authorised to make changes to it. Each area of the project is covered by one individual, and by a single document which is a record of design decisions made in that area.

This has clear implications about how the specification hierarchy of Fig 5.1 should be structured. In general it should follow the structure of the system itself, with a separate specification for each separate module. It should also follow the structure of the project team, with a single individual responsible for each specification. Several people may make contributions to one specification, but it is important for the future evolution of the design that there is one person who is *responsible* for that specification at any one time. Sometimes it may be necessary to transfer 'ownership' of the specification from one person to another; this should be done clearly and cleanly.

At any instant there should be not only a passive set of paper specifications, but an active group of individuals watching over each area who can assess, say, the effect of changes somewhere else. The two structures mirror and complement each other.

All this becomes more significant the larger the project is. On a small project, there may be a single specification covering the

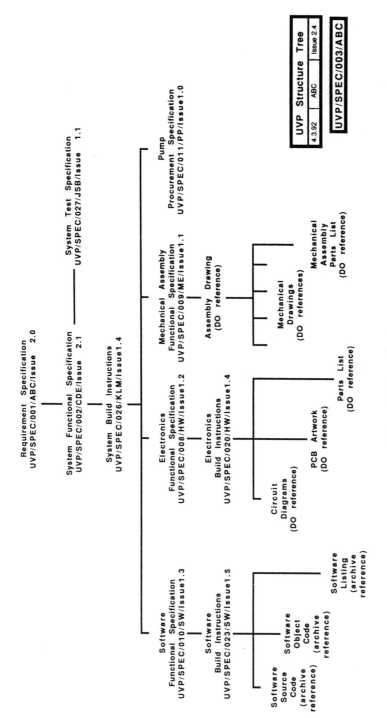

Figure 5.1 Specification tree

whole design. It is still important to define clearly the role of
each individual, and ensure that specification issues go through
a single channel which can assess the implications on the whole
project. On a large project, particularly if it is multi-site or
international, the whole edifice will collapse if there are not clear
and well understood procedures for handling specifications.

Specification changes

The owner of a specification should be the one person
authorised to change it. This does not mean that he or she can
make a change regardless of others' opinions. There are some
changes which only affect the internal implementation of a
particular module; but most have a wider effect, if only on the
timescale and cost of the project.

The specification owner is responsible for agreeing any
change with (a) the system designer and (b) all other
specification owners who will be affected by the change. In the
early days of a project, it is enough for this process to be
managed informally. As the design solidifies, and *any* change
becomes both costly and time consuming to implement, a more
formal authorisation process is appropriate. This might require
the signature of the system designer and/or the project leader.
The onus is then on the system designer/project leader to ensure
that all other specification owners have seen and approved the
change, and any implications on cost and/or timescale are
justified. The change control procedure described below is an
appropriate way to manage this.

The end result

Documentation – and specification in particular – is often seen
as an undesirable burden on development. Many designers and
engineers, and some project leaders, regard it as a chore and a
distraction from the 'real' work they are paid to do.

Apart from being unprofessional, this actually misses the
point of what development is about. Very few developments are
justified on the basis of producing a single working prototype.
Usually, whatever has been developed needs to be produced and
sold in hundreds, or thousands, or hundreds of thousands in
order to justify the whole exercise.

To make this possible, a manufacturer needs a set of detailed
production documentation that will allow him or her to build
whatever is wanted from a set of standard components and

materials. In a very real sense, the true output of development is a stack of paperwork (or, sometimes, computer tapes). The first steps in building this are a requirement specification, a functional specification and the other items of development paperwork. Documentation is a main line development activity, and a very useful skeleton round which to structure the whole development process.

DOCUMENT CONTROL

Paperwork is a very necessary part of development. Specifications, correspondence, meeting notes, reports, technical notes etc are all produced as part of the process. Some way to keep track of this mass of paperwork is needed without imposing too much administrative burden. This seemingly trivial problem is the cause of much frustration, lost information and poor communication. Appendix A describes a document control system which works well in practice.

MANAGING CHANGE

One of the most difficult skills of development is managing the process of change. Development succeeds by harnessing the creativity of individuals and making use of the latest advances in technology to produce the most cost-effective solution. But too much change, and *any* change for change's sake, slows down the whole process and leads ultimately to chaos.

At the start of the project a loose rein is appropriate, provided there is a clearly defined and well communicated goal. While the team is small and the design is on paper, changes cost little. As the project progresses to the development phase, tighter control is needed. With more people involved, and investment gradually built up in detailed designs, partly built prototypes and (not least) intellectual effort expended on a particular approach, any change becomes costly in both time and money. As the design becomes more solid, almost any change is likely to have ramifications in all areas.

Appendix B describes a change control system with a graduated degree of control, so that the screws can be tightened in stages as the project progresses. The system requires a minimum of administrative overhead, and works well in practice.

WORKING TOGETHER

Some company cultures are well set up to support development activity. Others are not. Whatever the company culture, it is up to the project leader to create a 'project culture' which works. In any creative activity, how people feel about what they are doing has a tremendous effect on their work. A 'just another job' attitude will produce just another product – or, more likely, just another failure.

Particularly at the start, a project needs to establish its identity. Team members may come from different departments or from different companies. They may be completely transferred to the project, or they may keep their position elsewhere, reporting to different bosses in a separate administrative structure. Wherever they come from, they should identify with the project and the project team as soon as possible. In the end, this comes from working together as a team. But there are ways of speeding up the process.

One of the simplest and most effective techniques is the use of physical space. If at all possible, a project team should sit together, or share an office, or take over a group of offices. The benefits of this are easy to see:

- Working relationships are built up much more quickly
- Loyalty to the project and the project team is rapidly developed
- Motivation is reinforced by the surroundings (rather than dissipated by other distractions)
- Communication takes place in minutes (by informal discussion) rather than days (by memo or arranged meeting)
- Misunderstandings can be cleared up before they take hold
- Chance discussions and overhearings generate new and useful ideas
- Team members immediately get the message that this project is their No. 1 priority.

All of this is difficult to quantify, but I would estimate that *not* locating a project team together adds at least 20 per cent to the cost of the project. In some cases the figure could be 50 or even

100 per cent. In this respect, being 300 yards apart can be nearly as bad as being in a different country.

Reasons advanced for not moving people together should be looked at in this light. Really, the only valid justification for not doing it is that either the project is very short term, or there is something else which is more important. Company culture is an important factor: if individuals feel they will lose their position in the organisation by moving somewhere else for a short period, they will avoid it if they can. Similarly, department heads may feel threatened if they see subordinates being moved outside their sphere of influence. They may also feel, quite legitimately, that long term working relationships, training or other work are being disrupted for the sake of short term benefits.

Project leaders may or may not have the authority to move people. Sometimes a deadlock with department heads results. Usually, it is worthwhile at a senior level in the company (a) to determine a general policy and (b) to evaluate individual cases. It is an important issue.

PURCHASING

In a product development, purchasing of components and equipment is often a difficult area. Purchasing departments in a manufacturing company are usually geared to buying large quantities of components at the lowest possible price, often to long term schedules agreed months in advance. Development teams, on the other hand, need very small quantities of components, and they need them yesterday. Simply following the standard ordering procedure – designed for high value orders which are carefully negotiated to obtain the very best terms – can be frustratingly slow. The cost of development purchases is often very small compared with the lost time of skilled personnel – not to mention the lost opportunity cost of a late development. Many development engineers prefer to do their own ordering, but this can upset buyers who have established long term relationships with particular suppliers.

This is a problem which needs to be brought into the open and resolved. Some companies employ a separate buyer for development, either within the purchasing department or within the development organisation. This almost trivial point of procedure can cause a great deal of delay, frustration, and heated argument.

Similarly, capital approval procedures in many companies are designed to handle items of plant equipment, which are carefully considered and costed well in advance. A development project, though, may need a piece of development equipment in a hurry to solve a problem which has only just arisen. Development equipment is often a fraction of the cost of production plant, yet it is often caught by the same capital net and has to go through the same procedures. The cost of not buying an item of production equipment (or delaying its purchase) may be, say, a few extra pence on the production cost of a particular item – a lot of money in the long term, but not a short term problem. The cost of not buying development equipment may be to arrive six months late in the market, which might be worth millions.

REVIEWS

The review is a useful mechanism to provide an independent view of how the project is progressing, and to assist the project team in identifying and suggesting solutions to problems.

Reviews can take many forms. A very successful format is a peer group review, carried out by a reviewer or a small panel of reviewers with relevant skills from elsewhere in the organisation. The review panel will ask questions of the project leader and key team members, based on their experience of similar projects and the problems they themselves have encountered. Often, a review panel can suggest solutions which might not have occurred to the project team, or can point out potential problems which may have been overlooked.

A review of this kind should have a touch of formality, but not too much. A degree of competitive feeling is appropriate, because the project team are exposing their professional skills to the judgement of their peers. However, if the project leader or the project team feel threatened they will adopt a defensive posture, and little will be achieved.

The atmosphere should be such that any member of the project feels able to state what worries them most. Project teams should see a review as a welcome opportunity to show what they have done, and to put forward unsolved problems for suggested solutions. Reviewers as well as reviewees can learn from the solutions adopted by the project team; this is a useful means of cross-fertilisation.

A general review of a project, covering aspects such as planning, budgets, key risks, review of requirements, and current problems, can be conducted in as little as two hours. A detailed technical review is likely to take longer, and may be most effective if it starts with a short presentation of the approach taken by the project team.

On a typical project, a general review can usefully be carried out at intervals of between one and three months. A full technical review, which may take a whole day or even longer, is worthwhile at key milestone points such as the end of a phase. While the project is running, a series of shorter technical reviews on particular subjects may be useful. One approach which works well during the design stage is to have a rolling technical review on a weekly basis, covering a different area of the project each week.

Ultimately, the review process should be seen as an aid to the project leader, in which everyone who participates is working together to ensure the project's success. It is the responsibility of whoever is running the review (and this is one case where the appropriate person is not the project leader) to create the right atmosphere.

A review session should always end up with a summary of key conclusions and identified actions. It should always be followed up with a written report, which may range from a one- or two-page summary to a detailed exposition.

A company which adopts a review policy can build up a series of checklists for different types of reviews. An example checklist for a software review is included in Appendix D. It is not necessary to follow checklists slavishly. The best approach is usually to state clearly the purpose of the review at the start (which often comes down to answering two or three basic questions), and then let it take its own course. The best value is generally obtained by letting reviewees speak what is on their minds. The checklist can be used as guidance to ensure that no key issues are forgotten.

External reviews

A peer review relies on having the relevant skills available within the organisation and not involved in the project. If this is not the case, a review can be carried out from outside. This is bound to be a more formal affair, and it is in the organisation's own interest to ensure that team members do not see it as a serious threat. External reviews, by people who have no background in the project and do not know the people or the organisation, are bound to take longer; but they can also give a broader perspective. For a worthwhile review, somewhere between a day and a week is likely to be necessary, depending on the size of the project, and how many reviewers are involved.

For this type of review, formal sessions in a large room are not usually the best approach. The most effective way is often to allow the reviewers to interview key project members on a one-to-one basis, and to walk round and observe development in action. Coming into a project from outside, some of the most informative comments can be obtained from the ordinary team members who are doing the work. If the organisation closes ranks and presents a united front, it will not get true value from the review.

Having invested in bringing an outside reviewer up to speed on the project, it is worthwhile to build on this by continuing the process on a regular basis. Once a reviewer has gained a basic knowledge of the project and knows the project team, a continuous review can be carried out by short visits at regular intervals. Such a review by an experienced person from outside provides senior management with an independent view, increasing confidence in the project, and can give some valuable suggestions to the project team. This arrangement works well in practice, and is particularly useful for any company new to development.

6 COST AND TIME

The foremost concerns of any organisation setting out on a development project are usually how much is it going to cost and how long will it take. Stories abound of development costs soaring out of control, or of a six-month project taking two years and costing five times the original estimate. The reality is rarely so dramatic, but it is a legitimate concern. How do you control the expenditure and the timescale on a complex development project?

The fundamental answer is: by controlling everything else. There is nothing done on a development project that does not affect the total expenditure. If a project budget is out of control, it is usually because of a problem in one (or more) of the areas discussed in the other chapters of this book. The solution lies typically in planning, or the assignment of responsibilities, or specification, or communication.

ESTIMATING

The only way to produce an accurate estimate is to base it on a project plan. A rule of thumb figure can sometimes be produced by simply listing what has to be done, but until you have drawn out a network plan it is impossible to be sure you haven't missed anything.

Like time estimates, cost estimates are best done in conjunction with the people who will actually do the work. This helps to establish goals and commitments, as well as giving more accurate figures. Realistic estimates are best made without any preconceptions of how much it *ought* to cost, or how much money is actually available. As in planning, delusions along the lines of 'this much money is available, therefore this activity will cost so much' are very easy to fall into. If the estimate does come out too high, then realistic steps can be taken to reduce it. But if the estimate is not real in the first place, an overspend is guaranteed.

'Five times the original estimate' stories are usually based on off the cuff figures produced at the idea stage of a project. Any assessment made early on is likely to be unreliable, and should be treated as such when planning finance. The phased approach allows estimates to be gradually refined as more becomes known.

A feasibility study should produce an 'order of magnitude' estimate for development cost, as well as an assessment of the business proposition, payback period and approximate cash flow. At this stage, the development cost is likely to have an uncertainty of 50 or perhaps even 100 per cent. However, in constructing a viable business proposition the development cost is often not the most significant factor.

Development is expensive, but the expense should be put in perspective. The total development cost for a consumer product often comes out roughly the same as the launch promotional budget. The development cost for any product will usually be dwarfed by the initial manufacturing expenditure. In most business plans, end product cost, markets and timing are far more significant for business success than a variation in development cost. This should be borne in mind when planning finance for a project.

It is advisable to make contingency plans for cash that are 50 per cent or even 100 per cent in excess of the projected development budget. Some projects end up paying more attention to cash limits than anything else. Yet reaching the market six months earlier, or adding a feature to distinguish from competition, can pay back many times over the extra development cost needed to achieve it.

Risk versus accuracy

The accuracy of estimating depends directly on the level of risk in the project. This in turn is closely related to the degree of novelty. The more innovative a project, the harder it is to produce an accurate estimate. This fundamental fact is one that no estimating technique can get round. All that good estimating can do is reduce the uncertainty to a minimum.

What estimating should do, however, is to get better as the project progresses. Producing a single estimate at the beginning of a project is useful, but only up to a point. Estimating becomes a worthwhile tool if it is followed through, with a regularly updated figure of the projected end date and projected cost of the project. This is not difficult to do if a plan is drawn, and is kept updated at regular intervals.

A history of estimated versus actual time and cost, together with current projections, is a very useful tool for judging how well a particular project is under control. A complex project with a high level of innovation might be expected to go through some difficult periods, especially in the early days. But if the historical figures show an increasing consistency in estimates and achievements, than it is likely that the project is well set up and is being gradually brought under control. If the projections fluctuate wildly (or, sometimes, if they stay the same despite major changes in fortune), and if short term estimates are consistently not met, then something is wrong.

Some understanding of the development cycle is important when interpreting estimates. Paradoxically, the most difficult part of a project to estimate is often the last part of the development phase. Feasibility studies are relatively easy to estimate; in fact, this is usually a case of setting a reasonable budget and then researching as deeply into the issues as the money and time will allow. The laboratory model is a little more difficult; but since this is only a model, it is not too difficult to leave out some features if the money starts to run out. This is a tendency to watch: sometimes it is appropriate to trade the results from a phase against the money and time available, but sometimes it simply stores up trouble for the future. If the laboratory model does not really get to the bottom of all the key issues, it can be a false economy.

The development phase, on the other hand, usually has a hard and fast goal which cannot be fudged. All the details which might have been overlooked before have to be in place at the end of development, and they have to work. This usually starts to hit home during the integration period, towards the end of the development phase (Chapter 2). Integration is where all the problems not thoroughly thought through during system design come home to roost. This is where the interfaces between modules which have been separately developed are put to the test for the first time. It is also where problems which have fallen down the cracks between different team members, or different sub-project teams, begin to emerge.

Often, the projected end date and cost will start to edge out as integration proceeds. This is not necessarily bad management. Neither is it bad management to be told that it is difficult to predict how long integration will take even though the end of the project is in sight. Integration is very frequently *under*-estimated. Estimating it accurately is extremely difficult, even when you are on top of it. This is the time when unknown problems appear, any of which may take a few hours or a few weeks to solve.

If integration does proceed smoothly, you can be sure that the project leader and the project team are well in control of the situation. Integration is made easier by doing a very thorough job during system design, and actively thinking through as the project proceeds all the things which *might* go wrong when the system is finally put together.

THE COST OF CHANGE

A fundamental fact of development is that, beyond the very early stages, *any* change costs money. Even a simplification in the design can end up costing more. Documentation has to be altered, hardware may need to be remade, and the implications on all areas of the project have to be thought through. This is rarely allowed for when estimating. In fact, one of the biggest enemies of accurate budgeting is the phenomenon of 'creeping enhancements': small features added here and there, none of which is significant in itself but which add up to a large effort. Much of this effort is simply managing the process of change and ensuring that inconsistencies do not creep into the design.

The solution is not to prohibit all changes – though many engineers would like to do that. There are many legitimate reasons for altering a design: new market pressures for example, or opportunities for cost reduction which have only just become apparent. What is needed is a standard way to balance the advantages of a change against the disadvantages, including the implications on time and cost of the project.

A change control procedure, such as the one described in Appendix B, provides this function. Where there are significant time and cost implications, the project leader should agree the change with senior management and adjust the budget and timescale accordingly. Assuming that changes will simply be absorbed without impact never works. The overspend happens anyway, and meanwhile the project ceases to be under control because it is shooting for an impossible target.

MANAGING COST AND TIME

Neither time nor money can be controlled directly. They are the result of many different factors, and can only be manipulated by careful juggling of the areas which *can* be controlled, such as planning and resourcing.

There are several ways of saving time:

- Use more resources
- Use better resources
- Overlap phases or activities
- Do more things in parallel
- Work longer hours/evenings/weekends
- Take more risks
- Relax the specification
- Relax cost constraints (development and/or product costs)
- Hire/buy better equipment.

Almost all of these involve spending more money. There are fewer ways of saving money:

- Work more efficiently
- Use less expensive resources
- Relax the specification
- Cut corners
- Cut overheads.

All in all, time is a lot easier to manipulate than money. Project costs obey a ratchet effect: almost anything you do to change the situation costs money, and changing it back costs still more money. If you list all the things that are likely to change during the course of a development project, and note how many of these are likely to *save* money, it is easy to understand why project costs have a tendency to move one way: upwards.

Time can often be saved by spending more money, but the relationship is not reciprocal. If a project deadline is very tight, relaxing it can save cost; but relax it too much, and the costs start to climb again.

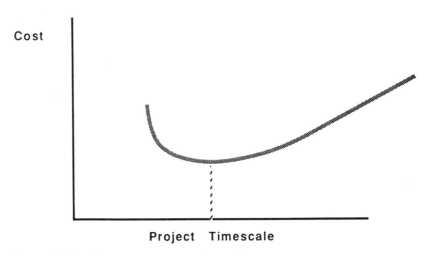

Figure 6.1 Development cost versus timescale

There are certain basic costs associated with keeping a project going – not least the cost of maintaining a team that actively understands every area of the design. Too relaxed a timescale also tends to dissipate effort, and leads to lapses of attention. With all other factors constant, altering the required timescale of a project has an effect rather like Fig 6.1. The minimum cost is likely to be achieved with a relatively short timescale – short enough to be challenging, but not to burn out the project team within six months.

What *is* possible is to stop unproductive spending. The best way to save money is by detailed planning in advance. This allows resourcing to be closely matched to the tasks required, and the most efficient resource to be planned in for each activity. Dependencies can be identified, and unproductive periods spent waiting for another activity can be reduced or eliminated.

Problems anticipated on paper are much cheaper than problems discovered at the last moment. Having made a plan, it should be followed, and kept up to date. If the situation changes, the plan can be reworked. The easiest way to increase costs is to let the project get out of control. Project teams have no difficulty spending money; it is up to the project leader to ensure it is spent productively.

An important method of limiting cost is to set clear time and cost goals for individual tasks. Parkinson's law applies to project finance: cost (and time) expand to fill the budget available – and, frequently, a little bit more. The 'little bit more' includes changes, unexpected difficulties and the problems that are not discovered until system integration. The corollary is that the project leader should choose time and cost goals which are tight but realistic, and then provide for some contingency. A challenging goal is a good motivator; a clearly unrealistic one is likely to be ignored. A goal that is too lax encourages procrastination.

Milestones

A single goal for the end of the project is rarely enough. Project cost, and time, are best controlled by setting a series of intermediate milestones. These should correspond to major achievements which are clear to all and, as far as possible, unambiguous, eg 'system design complete', 'circuit diagrams complete', 'software tested', 'integration test complete'.

Milestones should be derived from the project plan. This does not mean they should be read directly from it. Judgement needs to be applied to the dates shown on the plan, which are the *earliest* dates at which it is possible to reach particular points.

Milestones which are on the critical path *can* often be set at the earliest dates shown on the plan. This implies that nothing slips – or that if it does, steps will be taken to recover the loss. This is reasonable, since the small number of activities on the critical path can be given close management attention, and resources can be diverted from elsewhere if necessary.

Choosing the earliest possible date is not reasonable for milestones which are not on the critical path, and it is not necessary in order to achieve the required end date. Milestones here should be set somewhere between the earliest and latest dates on the plan – bearing in mind the point made in Chapter 4, that float is shared between tasks and cannot be used more than once.

Fig 6.2 shows a 'raw' plan with earliest start dates, and Fig 6.3 the same plan with milestones set. It is always necessary to reprocess the plan to ensure that setting particular milestone dates does not have undesirable effects in other areas of the plan.

Milestones should not be imposed from above without discussion. To be effective, they should be agreed with the person or persons responsible for achieving them. Sometimes, the formality of agreeing milestone dates in writing is useful. The important point is that whoever is responsible should take

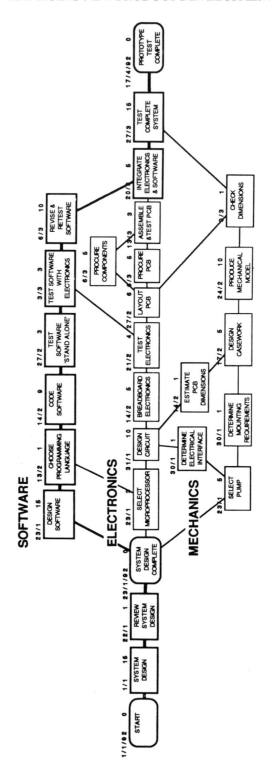

Figure 6.2 'Raw' plan

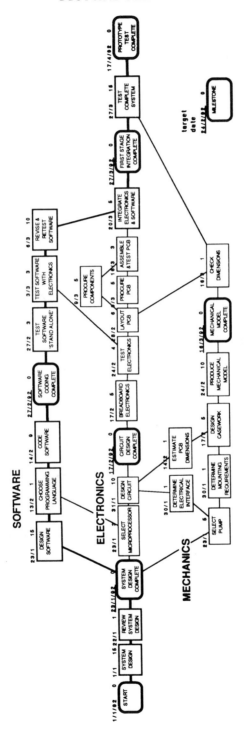

Figure 6.3 Milestones

up the challenge of achieving it, and 'own' that date as a personal target.

It should always be clear who has the prime responsibility for achieving any milestone. Ultimately, it is always the project leader; but on a large project he or she may delegate responsibility to a sub-project leader or a key project member.

Achieving the right attitude to milestones is an important factor in controlling costs and time. The best results are obtained where team members accept a milestone as a challenge and a matter of personal pride. Milestones should be discussed at progress meetings (see below). Achievement of a milestone should always be acknowledged, certainly to the rest of the project team and, where appropriate, to senior management or to the client. A milestone which is not achieved should become a focus of attention, and steps should be taken to understand why it has not happened and to resolve the problem. Sometimes, there are legitimate reasons. For example, resource may have been diverted to critical path activities. When the situation is understood, the milestone should be re-set.

Progress meetings

Progress meetings are an essential tool in keeping cost, time, and the direction of the project under control.

Fundamentally, a progress meeting has three objectives:

- To find out the state of progress in each area of the project (and hence to update the project plan)
- To identify any problems, and find ways to resolve them
- To set and agree goals for the immediate future.

The progress meeting is the basic mechanism by which the project leader can understand and influence the detailed course of the project.

There are many ways of running progress meetings. Sometimes it can work simply to walk round the project site and spend a few minutes with each team member discussing progress, problems and goals. A useful backbone for 'walk about' meetings like this is the project plan. The plan can be marked up to indicate progress in each area. The effect on other activities of, for example, a slip, can be clearly shown. The plan is a useful check that no areas of the project have been missed out.

Having collected all the information, it is worthwhile to reprocess the plan, and discuss any issues arising (for example, reprioritising of activities) with the people concerned. The plan can then be redistributed in its revised form. An exercise like this can often be conducted within a day.

On a small project, a weekly progress meeting can be conducted with all participants to ensure that all team members know what is going on. A week is usually the appropriate interval. A month is a long time in project management, and in project expenditure. Staggered meetings (see Chapter 5) work well on large projects, to keep the size of the meeting down. Progress meetings need a strong hand, to ensure they do not stray into discussing detailed technical issues, which are best addressed separately.

Progress meetings do not replace the duty of the project leader constantly to assess the critical activities of the project, and to identify and solve problems whenever and wherever they arise. But they do provide a regular formal check at intervals on *all* areas of the project, which can sometimes overturn some very unpleasant stones.

Progress reports
To supplement progress meetings, written reports are often useful. It is possible to go overboard on reports and spend a disproportionate amount of project time writing them. But a simple mechanism, which records the key facts without taking up project members' time, can produce worthwhile information.

Figs 6.4 and 6.5 show a report format I have used successfully on a relatively large project which incorporated a variety of technical disciplines and a number of sub-project teams. It is a standard form which is filled in by the sub-project leader on a weekly basis. Use of a form means there is no need to worry about how to lay out the report, and no need to get it typed. The format encourages concise descriptions of tasks, although there is a blank area to put down worries and problems.

The report format of Fig 6.4 is closely linked to planning. In this case, team leaders drew up and maintained their own plans. The activities listed should correspond to activity descriptions on the plan. The 'critical path' column identifies those activities which are on the current critical path for the team, and which should therefore be given priority. Estimated or actual

```
┌─────────────────────────────────────────────────────────┐
│                    WEEKLY REPORT                         │
│              FOR ............... PROJECT TEAM            │
│                                                         │
│                WEEK ENDING ................              │
├─────────────────────────────────────────────────────────┤
│  Forecast  completion  date                             │
│                                                         │
│     CURRENT:            LAST:          TARGET:          │
├─────────────────────────────────────────────────────────┤
│  Activities  completed  this  week      Critical  Path  (Y/N) │
│    •                                                    │
│    •                                                    │
│    •                                                    │
│    •                                                    │
├─────────────────────────────────────────────────────────┤
│  Activities  in  progress        Target  Completion  CP(Y/N) │
│    •                                                    │
│    •                                                    │
│    •                                                    │
│    •                                                    │
├─────────────────────────────────────────────────────────┤
│  Activities  planned  for  next  week  Target  Completion  CP(Y/N) │
│    •                                                    │
│    •                                                    │
│    •                                                    │
│    •                                                    │
├─────────────────────────────────────────────────────────┤
│  Changes  to  plan                                      │
│                                                         │
│                                                         │
├─────────────────────────────────────────────────────────┤
│  To  be  resolved                                       │
│                                                         │
│                                                         │
│                                                         │
│                          ....................Project  Leader │
└─────────────────────────────────────────────────────────┘
```

Figure 6.4 Weekly report

```
┌─────────────────────────────────────────────────────────┐
│                    WEEKLY REPORT                          │
│          FOR .TRANSPORTER. PROJECT TEAM                   │
│            WEEK ENDING  2/2/96                            │
├─────────────────────────────────────────────────────────┤
│ Forecast  completion  date                                │
│   CURRENT: 31/9     LAST: 10/10    TARGET: 1/10           │
├─────────────────────────────────────────────────────────┤
│ Activities  completed  this  week      Critical  Path  (Y/N) │
│  · DEBUG MATTER TRANSPORT SWITCH            N             │
│  · UPDATE ALPHA PARTICLE CONVEYOR           Y             │
│  · DESIGN NEW CONTROL PANEL                 N             │
│  ·                                                        │
├─────────────────────────────────────────────────────────┤
│ Activities  in  progress       Target  Completion  CP(Y/N) │
│  · DETERMINE MTBF OF PROTOTYPE        15/3        N       │
│  · TEST ALPHA PARTICLE CONVEYOR        4/2        Y       │
│  ·                                                        │
│  ·                                                        │
├─────────────────────────────────────────────────────────┤
│ Activities  planned  for  next  week  Target Completion CP(Y/N)│
│  · TEST MATTER TRANSPORT SWITCH        7/2        N       │
│  · BUILD SECOND CONVEYOR              15/2        Y       │
│  · MANUFACTURE CONTROL PANEL          11/3        N       │
│  ·                                                        │
├─────────────────────────────────────────────────────────┤
│ Changes to plan                                           │
│ Conveyor test taking longer than expected; manufacturing │
│ schedule revised to bring plan back on course.           │
│ DISINTEGRATOR sub-plan reworked.                          │
│ RECALIBRATE OPTICS added after IMAGER VIBRATION TEST      │
├─────────────────────────────────────────────────────────┤
│ To be resolved                                            │
│ Volunteers needed for MATTER TRANSPORTER TEST (12/6).     │
│ Specification needed for acceptable degradation in        │
│   reconstituted object.                                   │
│ Meeting to be arranged with Control System team.          │
│                              G. Brown....Project Leader   │
│                                  2/2/96                   │
└─────────────────────────────────────────────────────────┘
```

Figure 6.5 Weekly report (completed)

completion dates are given for each activity.

A report like this can be produced in less than an hour. It allows team leaders to acknowledge what has been completed in the last week (and compare it with what was predicted in the last report), and to set clear goals for new activities. Changes to the plan can be clearly specified, rather than drifting into existence with some people not aware of them. Any problems (whether technical, or due to resources or equipment, or arising from interaction with other sub-project teams) can be flagged early, while it is still possible to do something about them.

Sub-project progress reports are invaluable to the overall project leader, who can see at a glance whether the right activities are being given priority, whether estimates are being achieved or not, and whether the end date for this sub-project is stable or is drifting out of control. This is particularly useful where a project is being carried out at multiple sites, and the project leader is not always on hand to observe what is happening. The larger the project, the more important written reports become.

Of course, pieces of paper are not enough. It is essential to talk to the people involved, to see at first hand the problems they are experiencing, and to verify the accuracy of the reports. But reports do provide a structure of hard information on which to build an understanding of the project. They are a very useful background to any progress meetings, whether ' walkabout' or more formal. Wherever possible, reports should be timed to be available just before a progress meeting.

Management reports

It is useful for a project leader to provide regular reports to senior management, or to whoever is commissioning the project. Some companies require it; all projects benefit by it. It helps to focus management attention, and to highlight problems (of resourcing, equipment etc) which need to be solved outside the project. Issues of changes in requirements, altered timescales or revised costs can be raised in this forum.

Management reports can usefully be produced at monthly intervals. A weekly report is rarely necessary, and takes a great deal of project time. One effective format is to produce a short written report which is discussed by the project leader in a meeting with senior management. Appropriate contents for such a report are:

- An updated plan, with completed tasks clearly marked, and the critical path shown
- A list of achievements since the last report, showing progress against the previous estimates
- Activities and milestones for the future
- Significant changes in plans or technical approach since the last report
- Updated timescales and costs for the project
- A current review of the key risks and problems, with necessary actions (inside or outside the project).

It is not necessary to provide detailed technical information, except where it is essential to illustrate key risks, problems or achievements. A long report is much less useful than a concise summary. The above information gives the key facts about the project in an easily digestible form. Apart from the project plan, a list of half a dozen key points, or (if necessary) a paragraph of text should be enough to cover each of the categories listed.

It is up to the project leader to set up the right channels of communication with senior management and to ensure that the key points are understood. If this isn't happening, it is up to the project leader to resolve it.

TRACKING EXPENDITURE

Any project involves three types of expenditure: labour, materials and expenses. Different organisations have different ways of recording these items and different rules about how freely these figures are available.

It is worthwhile to plot a predicted expenditure curve for the project, and to superimpose the actual expenditure on a weekly basis. The result will look something like Fig 6.6. The S-shape arises because project expenditure starts out low, builds to a peak, and then (hopefully) tails off towards the end of the project. The S-curve is a cumulative plot; a plot of the weekly expenditure should look roughly like Fig 6.7, which also shows an approximate breakdown into the types of activity at each point in the project.

Also relevant, naturally, is achievement. This can be measured by progress against milestones. If the project is on budget but a

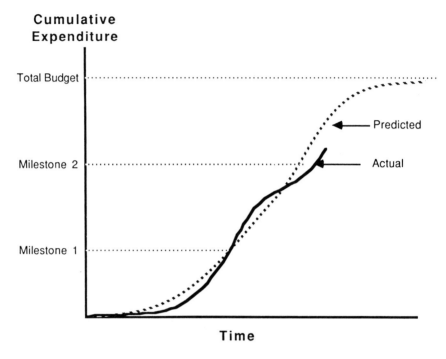

Figure 6.6 Expenditure curve

month behind schedule, then it is likely to overspend. If no more slippage occurs, then the amount of overspend can be predicted to be roughly one month's expenditure at the current rate. A plot like this is a worthwhile exercise for the project leader's peace of mind, and a useful adjunct to the management report.

Care must be taken in interpreting the expenditure curve, however. Materials and expenses, for example, are often paid in arrears. A major item of equipment, or an outside contract, can suddenly appear in the figures several weeks after the commitment was made.

The labour figures available to the project leader may be derived using many different accounting conventions. They may or may not include overheads; the rates may or may not include a recovery element. The convention does not really matter, as long as the estimate and actual figures are calculated in the same way.

As a general rule it is desirable that the figures available to the project leader should be as 'real' as possible. That is, they should

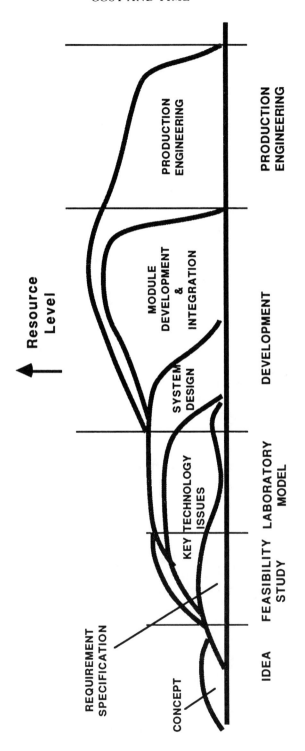

Figure 6.7 Key activities during development

reflect the true cost to the company. This is particularly important if internal resources have to be weighed up against the cost of using an external contractor. Artificial accounting procedures can lead to artificial decisions.

Some companies control time instead of money – for example, hours booked to the project. This is a valid method, but it does hide from the project leader the true cost of what he or she is doing. Often a more cost-effective solution is achieved by letting the project leader know what the true costs are, including the cost of labour. The real worth of a new piece of equipment that will double design productivity can only be measured if these figures are known.

If the project is assigned a full-time fixed team, then the labour cost is easy to work out: it is simply the weekly cost of the team multiplied by the number of weeks. This is one way of simplifying project management, and reducing all budget worries to the simple factor of time. The project leader's task is simply to complete the job in as short a time as possible. The disadvantage is that expert resource outside the project team is not available (although it might be subcontracted). There are, however, a number of advantages: a small, dedicated team quickly builds a strong team spirit, communication is easy, and commitment can be built up very quickly. It is also a satisfying way to work.

The sweatshop approach
There is an extreme form of this method, which can be characterised as the 'sweatshop' approach. Put simply, it consists of selecting a project team, putting them together in a room, giving them a clear goal and throwing away the key until the job is done. Often the team are given some personal incentives to complete within a certain time. With the right people, this can work, provided the participants are willing. However, making all the people fully available at the right time can be difficult – and someone has to pick up the pieces afterwards. The best sweatshops are those which arise naturally, driven by the enthusiasm of the project team.

Some organisations have tried setting up teams like this on a separate site with their own support facilities. The idea is to create an environment where the project team feels that everything is under their control and, conversely, everything depends on them. This is virtually setting up a separate small company. In some cases the project team have taken the hint and decided to complete the process of separation. It can be difficult to reintegrate a group like this back into the parent organisation when the project is over. But it is a good way to 'spin off' new enterprises on a trial basis, if that is what is wanted.

PRODUCT COST

There is another cost factor to take into account in any product development: the cost of the final product.

The attitude often taken to development is 'Make it work, then make it cheap'. Unfortunately, design decisions taken early on may be impossible to reverse, and may force a high cost solution. The way to avoid this is to ensure that the goal set *at the start* of development includes an explicit cost target.

Quality can be defined as 'fitness for purpose'. If a product is too expensive to meet the need for which it is intended, then it does not fulfil its purpose. It is lacking in quality. A Rolls Royce is not an acceptable solution for a Mini application. Engineers, however, naturally like to produce elegant solutions to problems. The project leader needs to ensure not only that the product is adequately engineered to perform its function, but that it is not over-engineered.

If designers are set the goal of reducing the cost of a product to a minimum, they will accept it and will often come up with some very creative solutions. If they are not set the goal, it won't be done.

It is worthwhile very early on in development to establish a cost breakdown for the product, including the cost of assembly and test. Assembly and setup procedures, and complex tests, can greatly increase product cost. In most cases, they can be designed out or at least simplified. An understanding of the production process helps in assessing this.

This product cost analysis can be tracked throughout development, and progress noted towards the cost goal. If it veers off course, explicit steps can be taken to correct it. It is a statistic every bit as important as the performance of the product, and in many cases will be much more important to business success than the cost of development itself.

7 UNDERSTANDING TECHNOLOGIES

MANAGING TECHNOLOGY

So far in this book I have said little about the characteristics of technologies themselves, except by way of giving concrete examples for planning and other techniques. Many of the methods of project management can be considered quite separately from specific technical issues. In fact a project leader needs to develop a certain perspective on technical issues (particularly in his or her own discipline), to avoid concentrating on detailed problems. A project leader's prime responsibility is for the project as a whole.

In the end, however, it is essential that any manager of a technical project develops a basic understanding of each technology involved, and particularly of those issues which are likely to affect the whole project. This does not mean becoming an expert. It does mean grasping the essential facts, understanding how the general pattern of development manifests itself in this particular technology, and developing an instinct for where the key risk areas are in each discipline.

The key knowledge needed in order to *manage* a technology is not quite the same as that required to work in it. There is a great deal of overlap, but the focus is different. By way of example I have set out below some of the key project issues that arise in two specific technologies −· electronics and software. The points listed here are intended to complement the detailed knowledge of the technology itself which must exist within the project team before any start can be made. Many of the issues described are of the type that affect the project as a whole, but do not necessarily prevent individual designers from carrying out what they see as their job. They are the issues that technical specialists sometimes forget in concentrating on their part of the project – especially when under pressure.

ELECTRONICS

Resourcing

Electronics is not one discipline, but many. A digital logic designer is likely to be of little use in developing a microwave radio. High speed digital processing is a very different world from low speed logic. Power supplies are an art form in themselves. Analogue electronics is a special type of skill. In selecting a project team, it is important to understand just what type of skill is needed, and to select the right people. A project leader without a background in electronics needs to take advice from an experienced engineer inside (or outside) the organisation who understands the issues and, preferably, knows the strengths and weaknesses of the people available. Most electronics engineers will 'have a go' at something new, and may do a good job, but this may not be enough for critical areas of the project. The first step, of course, is identifying at the planning stage just what type of skills are needed for each activity.

The development process

Fig 7.1 shows a general plan for electronics development. A circuit will typically be designed on paper, then built as a breadboard using prototype assembly techniques. After test and modification, a PCB (printed circuit board) will be laid out to carry the components.

PCBs are almost always used for production electronics: they are more reliable, and far cheaper in volume production. PCB layout is usually done by a draughtsman, under instruction from the circuit designer. Communication between designer and draughtsman is often a problem, especially when the designer supplies circuit sketches on scraps of paper with incomplete or illegible component information. The first step in PCB layout is usually for a clean copy of the circuit diagram (or circuit schematic) to be produced by the draughtsman, and checked and agreed by the circuit designer.

PCB layout all used to be done manually using adhesive tape on tracing film, but nowadays computer aided design (CAD) systems are increasingly common. Some CAD systems allow

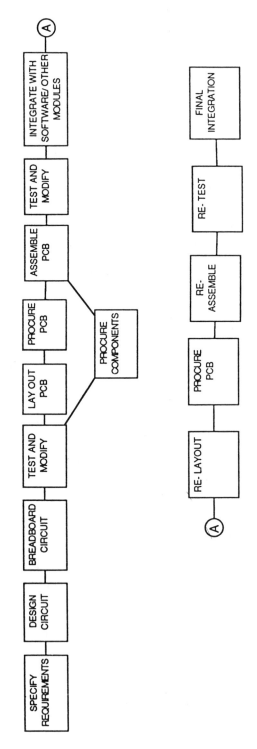

Figure 7.1 Electronics development

circuit schematics and component information to be entered and checked against the PCB layout. This is a tremendous help in avoiding errors. With a taped layout, it is important that the final layout is thoroughly checked against the circuit by draughtsman and circuit designer.

PCB manufacture is almost always subcontracted to a specialist company. PCBs can be obtained within 24 hours of supplying artwork – at a price. The price of PCBs depends critically on the turnround required. Development PCBs will cost several times the production price. To obtain the minimum price, it is necessary to allow several weeks. This implies that PCB design must be fixed some time before any volume production can begin.

Components for breadboard circuits are usually obtained from stock or as samples. When building PCBs (especially in quantity), it is usual to procure components explicitly. This requires planning, because some components may have a lead time of several weeks. Custom components (specially wound coils, for example) will need to be negotiated with the supplier, which again may take some time. The grey area between samples and production quantities is often a difficult time for procurement, and can cause serious delays if not managed carefully.

Once assembled, PCBs will be tested, and errors corrected by cutting PCB tracks and soldering new wires as necessary. Having tested the electronics in isolation, it needs to be integrated with the rest of the system. This may show up further problems. It is wise to schedule at least one PCB iteration – more if the circuit is layout critical, for example a radio or high speed logic.

Production issues
The most common problem in electronics development (apart from getting a circuit to work at all) is a design that works well on the bench but will not perform reliably in the thousands, or hundreds of thousands, that come off the end of a production line.

There are many more people in the world who know how to get a piece of electronics working than there are who understand how to produce a fully reliable design that can be made in quantity. The major problem is usually tolerancing: component values are never fixed, but vary in practice over a tolerance range. Having a system working on the bench is no guarantee that it will work with all combinations of supplied components, even if all the components are within their specifications. Getting this right requires long and painstaking calculations of worst-case combinations. Temperature must also be taken into account, since this affects component values.

Tolerancing needs to be done before an electronic product can be put into production. If the circuit has been developed by an experienced designer using good engineering practice, it may simply be a case of doing the necessary calculations and changing one or two component values to make sure that the circuit is always within specification. However, if a circuit relies on 'typical' rather than worst-case component timings and speed is critical, there can be serious problems. Having to swap components on a production line to find out which combinations work is a nightmare situation.

Sometimes, the situation can be resolved by using parts with a better specification. Otherwise, there may not be a simple solution. Occasionally component manufacturers can be per-suaded to select parts specially – at a price, and usually only for a large order. Some of the early personal computers relied on this for their operation, but production volumes were large enough to make it viable. The alternatives are a high reject rate on the production line (or even in the field), or else a redesign.

A far better option is to ensure that electronics designers are fully aware of the needs of production, and take tolerancing into account as a matter of course.

Component supply can be another source of problems – in production rather than in development. If a component is single sourced (ie available from only one supplier), the entire product depends completely on that supplier. If he or she has a run on that component, or stops making it, or goes out of business, production stops until the product can be redesigned. This is an all too common problem in electronics production.

The solution is always to use components which are available from at least two suppliers (dual sourced). This has implications on tolerancing, because the specifications of two different sources of components may well be slightly different. Established manufacturers usually build up a list of approved component specifications for their designers to use. Each specification will quote two or three suppliers, to simplify the job of the purchasing department.

Where there is no alternative to a single sourced component, it is wise to enter into discussions with the component manufacturer to ensure continuity of supply. All of this can be left until the product is production engineered; but a great deal of time will be saved if these issues are considered during development.

Noise

Most electronic circuits suffer from electrical noise – that is, pickup of electrical interference from mains or from other circuit elements close by. How serious this is depends on the particular circuit. Noise can mean that a circuit works most of the time, but very occasionally fails. This is a very difficult problem to track down. It is avoided by careful circuit design, by attention to the positioning of components on the printed circuit board, and by adequate decoupling and grounding of circuit elements. It is sometimes overlooked by logic designers, who are tempted to regard logic elements as perfect switches rather than electronic components susceptible to all the same influences as analogue electronics.

Noise can be a major problem in high speed logic circuits. It can sometimes be solved by, for example, adding extra power and ground layers to a PCB. But multilayer boards are expensive. The true art of electronic design is to solve problems in as cost-effective a manner as possible.

Manufacturing technology

Conventional electronic assembly uses components with leads which are inserted into holes in a PCB. This technique, however, sets a limit on component density. Higher densities can be achieved by using surface mount techniques. Surface mount components are 'leadless'. They have either pads or very short leads (see Fig 7.2), and are soldered to copper pads on the surface of the board.

The principal reason for using surface mount is to make smaller products. However, surface mount requires automated assembly, and this should in the long term be cheaper than conventional assembly techniques.

UK industry has been slow to catch up the lead established by Japan in this technique, partly because considerable manufacturing investment is required in surface mount equipment. However, this is starting to change.

Surface mount is definitely worth considering, since it leads to

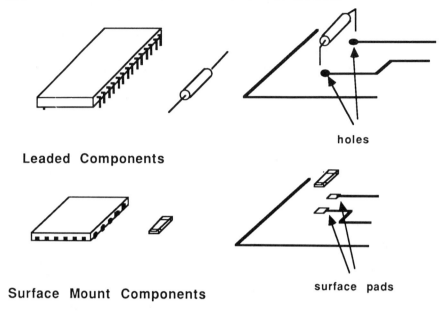

Leaded Components

holes

Surface Mount Components

surface pads

Figure 7.2 Surface mount components

smaller, neater products, as well as significant savings in PCB areas. Surface mount components started out more expensive than conventional components, but prices have fallen rapidly. In time, this is likely to become the standard assembly technique for electronic products.

Where the production volume justifies it, other techniques can be used. Tape Automated Bonding (TAB) and chip-on-board technologies are well worth investigating for mounting silicon chips in high volumes (hundreds of thousands).

Custom silicon

I have said nothing about the development of special purpose silicon chips – whether gate arrays, semi-custom or full custom. This is a technology in itself, with its own characteristics. (In fact, it shares many of the problems of software.) Special purpose silicon can dramatically reduce the cost, size and power consumption of any product which contains electronic logic and is made in quantities of a few thousand or more. It is also difficult to copy. Silicon development needs careful management and a degree of investment, but it is an excellent way to gain competitive advantage.

SOFTWARE

Software is in many ways the odd man out among technologies. Many of the rules which apply to a wide range of other disciplines are simply not applicable here. The difference, and most of the problems, arise from the fact that software is abstract. Software has no unique physical embodiment: it is simply a set of instructions to a computer. It may exist as a paper listing, on a computer screen, on a disk or tape, or as a pattern of bits in the memory of a computer. Such a slippery technology is difficult to deal with.

From a management point of view, the most difficult problem is that nothing is visible until very late in development. The progress of a mechanical device can be clearly seen; electronics can be observed at the breadboard stage and tracked through PCB layout, assembly and test; but a piece of software may not actually do anything observable until a very late stage. Unless something is done about it, project leaders may only have the programmer's word that anything is happening at all. Development may be 80 per cent complete before the software is really tried in anger. This is a poor moment for major problems to emerge.

The best solution is to manage software development, more than any other technology, in a disciplined way. Some project leaders resolve the issue by using a software designer they feel they can trust, and leaving the whole process entirely up to them. This can work, but it carries an inevitable risk. Even with this approach, it is necessary to define very clearly exactly what is wanted from the software.

There is a great temptation in software development to rush into programming at the start. However, program instructions, even in a 'high level' language, are really at too detailed a level to design a complex software system. This is rather like laying the bricks for a house without first having a plan for how everything fits together.

The project leader should ensure that first the requirements and then the software design are *written down*, understood and agreed before any programming takes place. This prevents false starts, and records the key intellectual work that has gone into designing the software system. After this, programming (or coding) should be straightforward.

The development process

A general plan for software development is shown in Fig 7.3.

The requirement specification is particularly important for software, since for a long while it will be the most concrete embodiment of what the system is supposed to do. There will rarely be any working model to try out and tinker with. It is often worthwhile to produce a separate software requirement specification which sets out in more detail exactly what is needed from the software.

The requirement specification describes *what* the requirements are, and should specifically exclude details of implementation. The next step is a software functional specification which states *how* the requirements will be achieved.

The software functional specification is really the top level of software design. It is appropriate to review it in some detail before going any further. Beyond this point, major changes to the structure of the software will be expensive.

Having agreed the top level, design can proceed to the detail. This involves taking each of the software functions already described, and turning them into a set of precisely defined procedures or modules. There are many techniques for this. An effective method is that of top down refinement. This entails taking each software function and splitting it into sub-functions, then subdividing these still further until a set of basic procedures is arrived at. Each of these can then be turned reasonably easily into program code.

There are several methods and notations available for detailed software design. One is to use pseudo-code, which combines short English descriptions of operations yet to be defined with precise logical structure. For example:

> IF temperature too low
> > THEN turn on heater
> > ELSE turn on fan;

The precise meaning of 'temperature too low', and exactly how to 'turn on heater' or 'turn on fan' have yet to be determined, but the structure is clear.

Other techniques use diagrammatic representations. There are complete software development methodologies (Yourdon method, Jackson method etc) which can be very effective. Some of these are detail design techniques. Others cover the whole

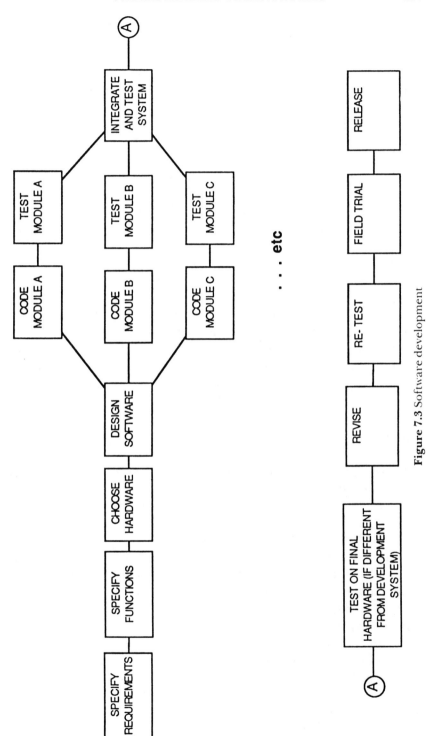

Figure 7.3 Software development

process of software development, from requirements analysis through to implementation. The important point is that *some* design technique should be used, rather than attempting to descend straight to program code.

If the software design has been done well, coding (or programming) should be a relatively straightforward, and reasonably short step. The hard part of software development is getting the logic right. This is best done without having to worry about the syntactic quirks of a particular programming language.

One aspect which should be considered at the functional specification and software design stages is how to test the software. A complex software system that doesn't work is extremely difficult to debug. The best solution is to test each module or procedure as it is written, then piece the system together in gradual steps, testing at each stage. This may require writing special software test harnesses, but it is well worth the trouble.

Having tested the software in isolation, it has to be integrated with the rest of the system. Integrating untested software with untested hardware is not the way to an easy life. A special test program may be needed to try out all the functions of the hardware before checking the full program. Again, the effort is well worth it.

Languages

A number of programming languages are available, and the software designer is usually faced with a choice. High level languages are designed for programming convenience and allow very much faster development, higher confidence in correctness, and a much easier task if any changes are required. Assembly language allows direct use of the hardware features of the processor and, if well written, takes less memory and is faster. However, it takes much longer to develop and requires a greater degree of skill. The low cost of memory means that in many cases high level language is the best option.

Each high level language has its own characteristics, and the final choice will depend very much on the intended application. For general applications, Pascal or C is a good choice. Pascal encourages good programming practice. Some experienced programmers prefer C because it allows more 'tricks' and short cuts. BASIC is good for getting something working quickly, but is not an appropriate choice for engineering a reliable system that is intended to have a long working life. Not all languages are available for all processors, of course, but the choice is rapidly widening.

The one case where the extra time, effort and skill of assembly language are really justified is where a program will be reproduced in tens of thousands 'burnt into' a memory chip. Here, extra bytes of software cost money. The extra effort required for assembly language should not be underestimated. Depending on the application, assembly language programming can take five times as long as the same application in high level language. Where the problem is simply one of program speed, it can often be solved simply by recoding a few small areas of the program in assembly language.

Standards and conventions
Wherever more than one person is working on a software project, there is a need for standards and conventions in the naming of procedures and variables, use of files, linkage conventions and so on. Someone on the project should be given the task of defining these at the start, and they should be adhered to throughout.

Reviews
Reviews are particularly important in the case of software. Since so many aspects of software development are hidden from view, it helps to bring them out into the open at intervals and have them looked over by an experienced software professional from outside the project. Chapter 5 discusses reviews in more detail.

Types of software
The term 'software' hides a great variety of techniques and applications. The simplest kind of application program is a straightforward list of instructions that takes data from input files, manipulates it according to some simple rules, and writes it to output files. The program determines exactly when it needs each item of data, and no unexpected events ever occur. This type of program makes no great demands on the capability of a computer, which is only designed to do one thing at a time. Most of the applications collectively referred to as 'data processing' (accounting, record keeping and similar functions) fall into this category.

Much more difficult is writing a 'real time' program which has to accept and respond to inputs from users, mechanical and electrical sensors and other devices occuring in any order and at any time. The program may have to interrupt what it was doing to service some unexpected request, then return to where it left off. It may need to keep several completely separate operations on the go at the same time. Since (parallel processors apart) a computer can only ever do one thing at once, this requires very careful design and programming.

There is a special type of real time programming called systems programming. This concerns the operating programs (called operating systems, or executives) which allow mainframe computers to handle several different applications programs of the data processing type at once. Systems programming is the most abstract branch of software, and requires a particular type of mind to do well.

Like electronics, software encompasses a range of different skills. The data processing community tends to divide software professionals into distinct categories. Systems analysts produce functional specifications and top level design. Application programmers carry out detailed design and coding. Systems programmers write operating systems. The three are rarely interchangeable. All are used to operating with 'standard' hardware – typically large mainframes from major manufacturers.

There is another type of software engineer with experience of writing microprocessor software for special purpose electronic equipment. These applications are usually real time, run on non-standard hardware and require a combination of both systems and applications skills: the ability to think abstractly and understand complex multitask interactions, with the capability to focus on very concrete application needs. Preferably, real time programmers should understand something about electronics hardware. This is a highly skilled job, and good software engineers with this type of experience are relatively rare.

The personal computer boom has also created a generation with the ability to program in BASIC and, sometimes, assembly language. These people are not afraid of computers; but, as with electronics, there is a world of difference between writing a short program in BASIC and creating a well-engineered, reliable software system.

In building a project team, the project leader should understand what he or she needs, and what he or she is getting. It is useful to have an experienced software professional on hand to give advice.

Estimating

Software estimating has a notoriously poor record. It is often all too true that the first 90 per cent of the work takes 90 per cent of the time, and the last 10 per cent takes 90 per cent again. Part of the problem arises from the fact that software is so abstract. Part is underestimating the time taken by testing and integration, which can be as much as half the total development time. Part is the effect of 'creeping enhancements'.

A project leader is wise to take software estimates with a pinch of salt and a hefty contingency, unless they are from an experienced professional with a track record of meeting schedules. The only way to arrive at an accurate estimate is to take a disciplined approach and compare with previous work of a similar nature. Even so it is wise to allow some contingency, and where possible to keep software off the critical path.

Team size

For simple tasks which can be clearly defined and require no communication, the time to achieve the goal can be shortened by adding more people. The situation is much more complex in development, and particularly in software development.

A particular software project usually has an optimum team size which is related to the number of parallel tasks the system can be naturally divided into. With fewer than the optimum, development will take longer because some of the tasks have to be done sequentially. With more than the optimum it can also take longer. Tasks may have to be divided up in unnatural ways. New members have to be trained and their work coordinated. The larger the team gets, the more problems of communication and management come to dominate, and the lower individual productivity sinks.

Project leaders – especially software project leaders – need to exercise their judgement in determining the right size of team for a particular task. This will usually become clear in working on the functional specification. They also need to keep their nerve when things start to go wrong: as Brooks states, 'Adding manpower to a late software project makes it later'. (Frederick P. Brooks, Jr., *The Mythical Man-Month*, Addison-Wesley 1975. This book is a classic on many issues of software development.)

Field trials

Field trials are particularly important for software. Because a software system is so complex, it is usually impossible for formal testing to cover all the possible combinations of use.

Software does not wear out, but it can exhibit some hidden features which only occur under very obscure conditions. For a piece of mechanics or electronics to operate at all, a large part of the design must be working correctly. With software, the fact that the system seems to work under normal conditions is no guarantee against a serious error lurking in some obscure corner of the code. The only way to guarantee correctness is to try all the options.

Field trials also test out the user interface. Where possible, they should be done with a draft user guide, and with a cross-section of users who have not been exposed to the product. First time users may struggle with some aspect of operation that is obvious to designers used to computers and software who have lived with the product for some months.

Some people have the right sort of mind to ferret out bugs in a piece of software. They are useful to know when it comes to field trials. Many people are pleased at the chance to try something out in advance of release. Students often do a good job of field testing. However, the field trial should also include users representative of the intended market for the product.

When setting up field trials, it is useful to supply a standard form for reporting any problems which arise. This should specify the circumstances of the fault as precisely as possible; which versions of software and hardware were in use; any other equipment which was being used with the system; and whether the fault is intermittent or repeatable. Monitoring the rate at which faults are reported is a good gauge of when the product is ready to be released.

Many companies release 'beta test' versions of software for use by friendly customers some two to three months in advance of the public launch date. This allows bugs to be identified and fixed before there are too many systems in the field. Many organisations are very willing to act as beta test sites. It is far better to delay release to allow proper beta testing to take place. Using the first batch of customers as beta test sites without their knowledge is not the way to establish a good reputation.

Version control

Trying to support several different versions of software in the field is a nightmare, particularly when a range of products is introduced. The number of possible combinations multiplies with every new version. Simply testing that everything works with everything else takes a great deal of time.

Part of the answer, of course, lies in thorough testing before release so that upgrades are not necessary to fix problems. Strict version control on software is essential, both during development and especially after release. Whenever a piece of software is changed, the version number should be raised, and this should be recorded in the source text. With a system comprising a number of separate modules, it is necessary to keep track of which version number of Module A works with which version of Module B, and so on.

Where possible, it helps to keep a record of which customers have which versions of software. This greatly assists in providing technical support and in supplying the correct versions of new products. It also helps if the software in the field is kept as up to date as possible. If a new product only has to work with the latest versions of all the other products, the problems of design and test are greatly reduced.

The best approach to this depends very much on the number of customers. An method which works for a hundred customers is unlikely to hold good for a customer base of ten thousand. Some companies offer a free upgrade to all customers, or an upgrade to all those who purchase a maintenance contract. Others operate an exchange service at a reduced price. This is a commercial decision, but one which is very much bound up with technical factors.

NEW TECHNOLOGIES

Knowledge about an unfamiliar technology is acquired in several ways: by talking to experts in the technology, and to project leaders who have managed it. Once experience has been gained in two or three technologies it becomes easier to see what key factors should be looked for in any new area. Always, it is necessary to work with experts in the technology and to give sufficient free reign to allow creative solutions.

But a project leader needs to maintain a perspective which

sees all problems in the light of their effect on the project as a whole. Keeping the right balance is a matter of judgement. The final verdict on whether you have it right is the end result.

Appendix A
DOCUMENT CONTROL

The problem of controlling and updating documentation increases rapidly with the size of a project; but even on small projects it can be a major headache.

On many projects, the burden is on individuals to keep the documents which are relevant to them, and to make sure they remain up to date. Or a standard company filing procedure may be used which is not designed for development, and proves unwieldy when faced with the special needs of a development project.

The method described here is simple to set up, and in practice it has proved easy to persuade project members to use it. The administrative overhead is very low, yet it provides an instant reference to all documents available on a given subject, and an up to date check on the latest versions of each. It can be used in parallel with other company filing systems.

The first step is to establish a central set of files *for the project*. The next is to set up a document register which is an index to all paperwork produced on the project. This index subdivides documents into categories such as correspondence, administration and specifications, and assigns a unique sequence number to each. Any document can then be referred to by a unique reference – for example:

UVP/SPEC/008

'UVP' is an abbreviated identifier for the project – ie 'universal vacuum pump'. 'SPEC' is the category – 'specifications'. '008' is the document reference number. Separate sequence numbers are maintained for each category, so that UVP/TECH/008 is a different document.

This reference uniquely identifies the document, but it is

useful to add other information for a full reference. For example:

UVP/SPEC/008/GPFV/Issue 2.0

'GPFV' is the author's initials; 'Issue 2.0' is the revision level of the document.

The entry in the document register provides in summary form all the key information about the document, for example:

Reference	Author/ Originator	Date	Title/Issue No.
UVP/SP EC/008	GPFV	20/01/92	Electronics Specification, Issue 1.0
		23/01/92	Issue 1.1
		04/03/92	Issue 2.0

Since the sequence number is unique, it is not necessary to quote the date when referring to the document. If the issue number is left out of the reference, the latest issue should always be assumed.

Whenever a new document is written, the originator should enter it as the next number in the register in the appropriate category, and ensure that the correct reference number appears on the document. A copy of the document should also be placed in the central project files. This takes only a few moments, and is all that is necessary to maintain the system.

The document register can be implemented as a text file on a word processor, or simply a central log book. The only requirement is that there should be a single, central place from which document numbers are allocated and where the status of all documents is recorded.

Categories which have proved useful in running projects include:

COR   Correspondence
ADMIN   Administration/management
MN   Meeting notes
SPEC   Formal specifications
TECH   Technical notes
CR   Change requests (see Appendix B)

It is wise to keep the categories simple and few in number to prevent any uncertainty over where a particular document should be filed. Categories should always be clearly defined.

Distribution

The document register ensures that documents are centrally recorded. A separate problem is ensuring that documents (and changes) are circulated to all the right people. A standard project circulation list is useful, from which team members who do not need a particular document can be crossed off. To prevent unnecessary circulation of paper, a two tier circulation system can be used. Names on a standard list which are not crossed off will receive a copy of the front page of a document only, to alert them to its existence; names which are circled or underlined will receive a full copy. Those with only the front page can, of course, obtain a copy from the project files simply by using the reference number. It is a good practice to insist that all documents carry a brief summary, as well as the title, on the front page.

It is a wise precaution to establish the convention that documents are only ever removed from the central files for copying, and are immediately returned. Team members can, of course, establish their own personal files of the documents most relevant to them.

Changes

Changes to documents must also be recorded. A common problem in development is that specifications (for example) are changed, but old copies still exist and may lead to significant errors.

The way to control revisions to documents is to ensure that every piece of paper on the project (apart from those unlikely to change, such as letters and meeting notes) carries an issue level. The issue level should be raised whenever any document is reissued. A two digit issue level provides scope for distinguishing between minor revisions (eg Issue 1.0 to 1.1) and major changes (Issue 1.1 to 2.0). Development documentation will normally start at Issue 1.0, although *production* documents (such as mechanical drawings and printed circuit board layouts) are often specified at alphabetic level during development (Issue A, Issue B etc) and only raised to Issue 1 on release to manufacture.

Reissues of any document (particularly specifications) must

always be recorded in the document register, and new copies circulated to the people affected. Team members should be encouraged to throw away superseded documents; they can always be referred to in the central files.

The change request system (see Appendix B) provides a means of controlling and circulating minor changes to a specification without reissuing the whole document.

Multisite projects

The system can be adapted for use on multisite or international projects, where it is difficult for everyone to access a common document register to obtain a unique sequence number. The simplest method is to add a site code to the sequence number, with each site maintaining its own separate set of sequence numbers within each category:

UVP/SPEC/B025/JSB/Issue 1.3

where 'B' is the site identifier. The separate document registers can be merged at intervals, and circulated to all participants.

Appendix B
CHANGE CONTROL

Most change request systems are designed to operate in a production environment. Usually a number of different forms are involved (engineering change note, engineering change request etc). It may take several weeks and a number of different signatures for a change to be processed through the system.

During development, however – particularly early development – systems like this are unwieldy and unnecessarily bureaucratic. If such a system is introduced, either it slows development activity to a crawl, or, more often, it is sidestepped. Yet it is necessary, particularly with a large team, to keep track of the current state of design, make sure all the necessary issues are considered when making a change, and communicate what has been decided to everyone who is affected.

The system described here uses a single form (Fig B.1), with four different status levels. The form can be used to raise an issue for discussion, or to notify an approved change. All changes are centrally recorded, and change requests can be periodically gathered together to update the formal documentation. The system operates as follows:

1. A CR (change request) may be raised by anyone at DRAFT status, simply by filling in the form and circling the DRAFT status at the top. This is an issue for discussion, and may be circulated to anyone on the team. At this stage it has no force of authority.
2. In order to move beyond the DRAFT stage, a CR must be approved. The approval procedure can be designed to meet the needs of the project, and it can be adjusted to provide the degree of control appropriate at each stage of development. Early on, it may be sufficient that the CR is signed by the sub-project leader(s) of all the modules affected. At a later stage, the

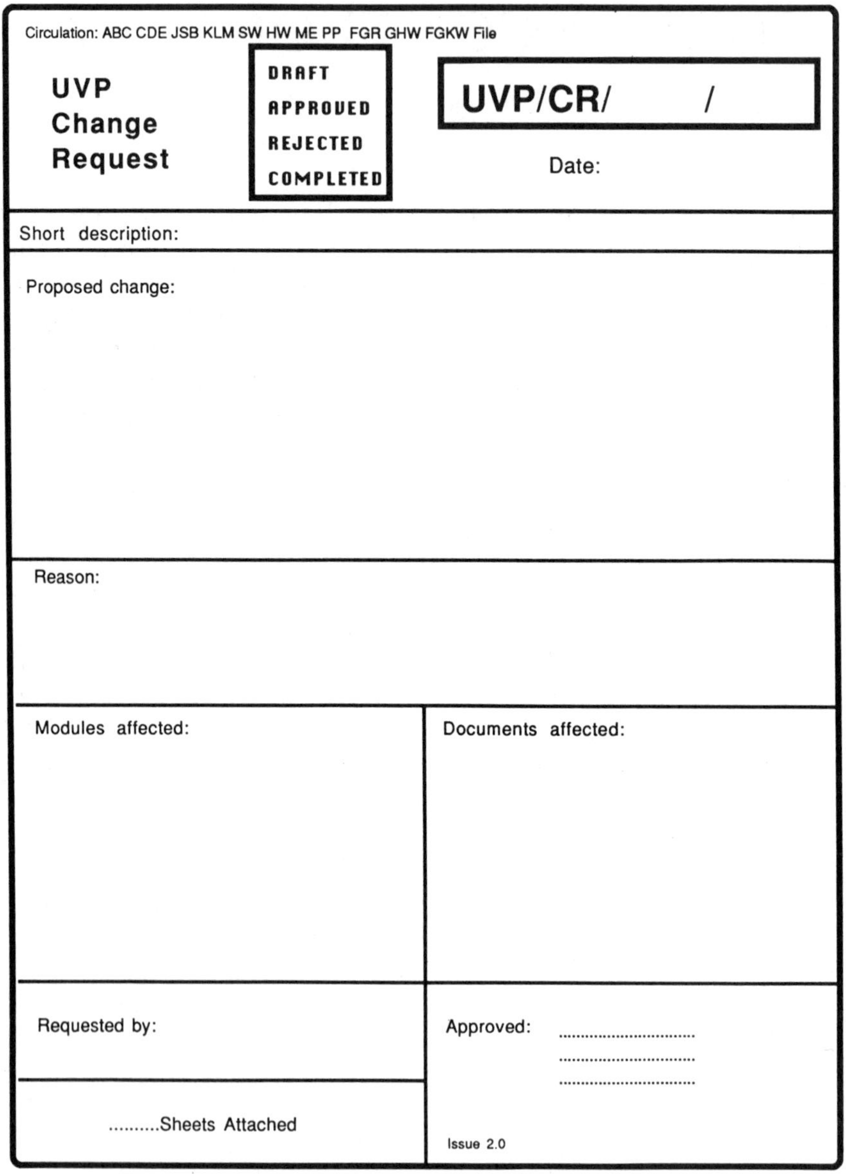

Circulation: ABC CDE JSB KLM SW HW ME PP FGR GHW FGKW File

UVP Change Request

DRAFT
APPROVED
REJECTED
COMPLETED

UVP/CR/   /

Date:

Short description:

Proposed change:

Reason:

Modules affected:

Documents affected:

Requested by:

Approved: ....
....
....

..........Sheets Attached

Issue 2.0

Figure B.1 Change request form

approval procedure can be changed to require the additional signature of the system designer or project leader. Towards the end of the project, any change may require the approval of the project leader, system designer and product engineer together. Whoever gives final approval should ensure that everyone on the project team who has a relevant opinion has been consulted.

Having obtained the required signatures, raising a CR to APPROVED status simply requires crossing through DRAFT and circling APPROVED. It should then be circulated to everyone affected. An APPROVED CR has immediate authority.

The different sections of the form cover the key issues which must be considered for any change:

- Proposed change. A clear description of the suggested change. Additional sheets may be attached containing sketches, marked up drawings, experimental results or other backup material.
- Reason. The reason(s) behind the proposed change. This may be anything from technical necessity or an error or inconsistency in the specification, to potential cost saving, an improvement in reliability or a new requirement suggested by market research.
- Modules affected. The modules or design areas which will be affected by the proposed change. A CR should always be circulated to the person or persons responsible for all areas affected.
- Documents affected. The documents (specifications, drawings, parts lists etc) which will need to be altered to reflect the change. This is an important reference for incorporating the change into the formal documentation.

CRs may prompt meetings or discussions to consider the issues raised. Depending on the number of CRs raised and their urgency, it may be worthwhile to organise a regular (say, weekly) meeting to discuss and progress outstanding CRs.

A central record must, of course, be kept of all CRs in force. This can easily be done through the standard document control system (see above). On raising a CR of any kind, it is assigned a number from the document register (eg UVP/CR/034). The register records the originator, short title, date and status (DRAFT etc, in place of issue level). A copy of the CR should be placed in the central project file. Whenever the status of a CR changes, this should be recorded in the register and a new copy filed, with signatures etc as appropriate. The register then records all CRs in force, as well as those still pending.

The use of a single form minimises the effort necessary to run the system. A CR can be amended on its way from DRAFT to APPROVED, but it is not necessary to write the whole story out again to implement the change. If major amendments are needed, or two or more CRs are to be incorporated into a single change, the original CR(s) can be REJECTED and a new APPROVED CR raised. The system is flexible enough to allow an unknown problem to be highlighted, or a detailed change to be proposed.

An APPROVED CR is really an advance notice of a formal change to one or more specifications. A change can be fully recorded, approved and circulated to the whole project team in less than an hour, without the need to reissue a complete specification. Periodically, the system should be tidied up by reissuing specifications to incorporate outstanding CRs. This is the purpose of the COMPLETED status on the CR form: a COMPLETED CR has been incorporated in a reissued specification, and has therefore been superseded. Fig B.2 shows the possible life histories of CR forms.

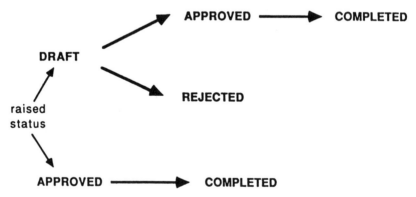

Figure B.2 Allowable life histories of CR forms

Limitations

The system described here has been designed for development use. It is not really appropriate for use in production. Production change control systems usually treat a change request form simply as notification of a problem, which can come from any area of the company including manufacturing, sales and field service. Manufacturing, for example, may request a concession to substitute one part for another because the part specified is not available.

Change requests are then evaluated by a committee which is likely to include representatives from development, manufacturing, sales and marketing. Requests are often grouped together, and submitted to a detailed evaluation including cost of implementation, urgency, and schedule of introduction (eg next production batch, immediate production, existing stock, or field recall). Approved changes are then written out as either a change note, which is a detailed instruction to a drawing office to change production documentation, or a concession direct to the factory. Changing a product which is already in the field is a much more difficult process and requires more complex systems than that described here.

Appendix C
FUNCTIONAL
SPECIFICATION
CHECKLIST

The following is a checklist for the typical contents of a functional specification.

Introduction
- Background, intended application (reference to requirement specification)

System overview
- System structure (diagram)
- Major subsystems
- Design principles

External interfaces
- User interface
- Other external interfaces
- Compatible equipment

System function
- Detailed operational description

Subsystem description
- Functional requirements for each subsystem

Subsystem interfaces
- Detailed description of each subsystem interface

Environment
- Operating environment (temperature, shock, vibration etc)

Test strategy
- Approach to testing
- Test plans
- Acceptance criteria

Appendix D
REVIEW GUIDELINES

The following is an example set of guidelines for a software review intended to take place at a particular point in a project. Similar guidelines can be developed for reviews at other times and for other purposes.

SOFTWARE
FUNCTIONAL SPECIFICATION REVIEW

Timing
This review should be carried out on completion of the software functional specification. It is the first major review of a software project.

Purpose
The purpose is to establish that:

- the requirement specification has been turned into a workable functional specification
- the functional specification interprets the requirements correctly
- functions are clearly separated and well defined, with minimum interdependence
- interfaces are clearly defined
- the user interface is clearly specified
- possible requirement changes have been anticipated and allowed for
- appropriate plans have been made for the next phase of the project

The aim of the reviewer should be to support the software

project leader in achieving the required aims. If problems are discovered, the reviewer should seek ways of advising or assisting the software project leader to overcome the difficulty. This is not a performance review, and no grades will be awarded.

Required documentation
- requirement specification
- software functional specification

Preparation
Before the review, the reviewer should read through the above documents. He or she should ensure that the software project leader is aware of the purpose of the review, and will be prepared.

Review checklist
- Go through the requirement specification. Clarify any points that are ambiguous, and allow the software project leader to explain exactly what the customer needs.
- Go through the functional specification. Consider alternative approaches, and talk through the consequences. Verify that all the requirements are satisfied.
- Ask what changes in requirements are possible, and how the design would be revised to cope with them.
- Review the interface specifications. Ensure that all aspects are, or will be, covered.
- Review the user interface. Does it meet the user's requirements? What degree of user friendliness will the customer expect, and does the design provide it? How robust will the user interface be, in the face of unexpected input? What type of user will be operating the system, and is the type of interface chosen appropriate to him or her?
- Ask the software project leader to explain his or her intentions for the next phase of the project. Consider especially:

    - the importance attached to design (versus coding)
    - proposed design methodology (if any)
    - method of structuring the design
    - how module divisions will be determined
    - methods of defining and organising data
    - notations to be used (eg graphical)

- conventions to be adopted
- how the design will be documented/recorded
- test plans

If there will be more than one team member in the next phase, consider:

- how the work will be split
- what steps will be taken to ensure adequate communication (eg regular meetings)
- how interface definitions will be handled
- team conventions

Prompt for the above information if necessary.

Feedback
At the end of the review, ask the software project leader:

- if the review has been useful
- if he/she intends to do anything differently as a result of the review
- how the review procedure could be improved

Record any comments.

Report
Write a report, to be circulated to the software project leader, the overall project leader (if relevant), and management as appropriate. The report may be free format, or on a standard form.

Appendix E
REQUIREMENT
SPECIFICATION

The following is a checklist for the typical contents of a requirement specification.

Introduction
- Background, intended application
- Intended market

Function
- Overview of function required

Features
- Detailed description of key features (including user interface)

Product range
- Product variants

Physical characteristics
- Size, weight, format, power etc

Environmental requirements
- Temperature, humidity, shock, vibration, weatherproofing etc·

Compatible equipment
- Units this product is designed to work with.

Detailed implementation tradeoffs are rarely understood when a requirement specification is first written. It is sometimes useful to indicate the relative importance of features by classifying them under three headings – *essential, desirable* and *nice to have*. These should be clearly defined, for example:

- Essential   key to the product concept
- Desirable   implement if minor impact on product cost, and reasonable impact on development cost/timescale
- Nice to have   implement if no impact on product cost, and minor impact on development cost/timescale.

Index

Note: Diagrams are shown in italic numbers unless there are textual references also on these pages.